A BIBLIOGRAPHY OF

AMERICAN DOCTORAL DISSERTATIONS

IN LINGUISTICS

1900 – 1964

COMPILED BY PHILLIP R. RUTHERFORD

WASHINGTON, D.C.

CENTER FOR APPLIED LINGUISTICS

1968

PREFACE

SO MUCH KNOWLEDGE has been acquired in linguistics in the
last half century that a serious dissemination problem has
occurred, and nowhere does so much valuable information lie
buried as in doctoral dissertations. Due to the general
inaccessibility of these scholarly studies, few people, even
those vitally interested in the field, know what exists; con-
sequently, much of this original research lies dormant and
is doomed to be repeated. This bibliography serves as an
attempt to acquaint scholars with what investigations have
already been completed and where they might be obtained.

Although I have endeavored to make this bibliography as
exhaustive as possible, I am not so naive as to think that
all dissertations in linguistics from 1900 to 1964 have been
included. There are no doubt some glaring omissions and some
questionable inclusions. I felt, however, that it was better
to err by being too inclusive than too exclusive. Some dis-
sertation titles which do not seem to be linguistic in any
sense are included because the abstracts, or other available
information, indicate they are at least somewhat linguistic
in nature.

As far as was possible, the entries were checked against
at least two sources to verify all information; due to the
nature of one source, however, there is a possibility that a
few of the dates could be off by one year. If a mistake is

encountered, the date should be almost invariably one year
prior to that given.

For their invaluable aid in the compilation of this
bibliography I thank Professors Fred A. Tarpley, Lawrence M.
McNamee, D.C. Butler, Bob Dowell, Charles E. Linck, and
Edna B. Stephens of East Texas State University. Also I
express my gratitude to Frank A. Rice and staff members of
the Publications Section of the Center for Applied Linguistics
for their assistance in the preparation of the manuscript for
publication and for providing an index.

Phillip R. Rutherford
Gorham State College
Gorham, Maine

March 1968

BIBLIOGRAPHY

BIBLIOGRAPHY

1 Aarsleff, Hans C. The study of language in England, 1780-1860. University of Minnesota, 1960.

2 Abbott, Orville L. A study of the verb forms and verb uses in certain American writings of the seventeenth century. Michigan State University, 1953.

3 Abboud, Peter F. The syntax of Najdi Arabic. University of Texas, 1964.

4 Abdalla, Albert G. An instrumental study of the intonation of Egyptian Colloquial Arabic. University of Michigan, 1960.

5 Abel, Arthur H. Aelfric and the West-Saxon Gospels. University of Pennsylvania, 1962.

6 Abel, James W. A study of the speech of six freshmen from Southern University (Negro). Louisiana State University, 1950.

7 Abernathy, Robert H. The structure of Russian roots. Harvard University, 1951.

8 Aboul-Fetouh, Hilmi M. A morphological study of Egyptian Colloquial Arabic. University of Texas, 1961.

9 Abramson, Arthur S. The vowels and tones of standard Thai: Acoustical measurements and experiments. Columbia University, 1960.

10 Ackerman, Ella L. Photographic study of the action of the velum palatinum as related to the velar sounds [k] and [g]. University of Ohio, 1934.

11 Adams, Arthur. The syntax of the temporal clause in Old English prose. Yale University, 1905.

12 Adams, Eleanor H. Old English scholarship in England from
    1566-1800. Yale University, 1914.

13 Adams, George C.S. Words and descriptive terms for 'woman'
    and 'girl' in French and Provençal border dialects. Uni-
    versity of North Carolina, 1950.

14 Adams, Sister Miriam A. The Latinity of the letters of
    Saint Ambrose. Catholic University of America, 1927.

15 Aguas, Estrello F. English composition errors of Tagalog
    speakers and implications for analytical theory. Univer-
    sity of California at Los Angeles, 1964.

16 Aiken, Janet R. Why English sounds change. Columbia
    University, 1929.

17 Al-Ani, Salman H. Phonology of Contemporary Standard
    Arabic. Indiana University, 1963.

18 Albright, Robert W. The international phonetic alphabet:
    Its backgrounds and development. Stanford University, 1953.

19 Albright, Ruth N. The Vedic declension of the type vṛkis:
    A contribution to the study of the feminine noun-declension
    in Indo-European. Johns Hopkins University, 1921.

20 Alexander, Luther H. Participial substantives of the -ata
    type in the Romance languages, with special reference to
    French. Columbia University, 1911.

21 Alexis, Joseph E.A. Concerning the German relatives after
    neuter substantivized adjectives, pronouns, or antecedent
    clause, and concerning the German indefinite relatives in
    eighteenth century prose. University of Chicago, 1918.

22 Algeo, John T. Aelfric's The Forty Soldiers: An edition.
    University of Florida, 1960.

23 Allen, Harold B. Samuel Johnson and the authoritarian
    principle in linguistic criticism. University of Michigan,
    1941.

24 Allen, Joseph D., Jr. Word formation with suffixes in
    Portuguese. University of Pennsylvania, 1940.

25 Allen, Robert L. The verb-system of present-day American
    English. Columbia University, 1962.

26 Al-Toma, Salih J.   The teaching of Classical Arabic to
    speakers of the Colloquial in Iraq. Harvard University,
    1957.

27 Alvarez, Atagracia.   Toponimos en los apellidos hispanos:
    un estudio onomástico. University of Southern California,
    1962.

28 al-Yasin, Izz-al-Din.   The lexical relations between
    Ugaritic and Arabic. Princeton University, 1950.

29 Ananthanarayana, Hallimysore.   Studies in the language
    of the Taittirīya Brāhmana. University of Texas, 1962.

30 Anantham, Sundur.   A study of the pronunciation problems
    involved in the teaching of English to Telugu speakers.
    University of Michigan, 1959.

31 Anderson, George K.   A study of case syntax in some Old
    Northumbrian texts. Harvard University, 1925.

32 Anderson, George M.   The use of language and rhetoric in
    Thomas Nash's The Unfortunate Traveller. Yale University,
    1961.

33 Anderson, James M.   A structural account of the evolution
    of intervocalic consonant clusters in Spanish. University
    of Washington, 1963.

34 Anderson, Llewellyn K.   The Bafia language: A preliminary
    statement. Princeton University, 1935.

35 Anderson, Ralph D.   A grammar of Laz. University of
    Texas, 1963.

36 Andreini, Christina B.   An analysis of the speech activi-
    ties of the aboriginal Maori of New Zealand. University
    of Southern California, 1950.

37 Andrews, David K.   The Aramaic relative particle DÎ and
    the problem of translation to Greek. University of
    Chicago, 1943.

38 Andrews, Nita.   A lexicographical study of the early
    French farces. University of North Carolina, 1942.

39 Andrews, Schofield, Jr.   The nasal present and the aorist
    in the Rig-Veda. Harvard University, 1961.

40 Andrus, Lawrence R. A study of subjunctive usage in the
    Roman de Troie. Cornell University, 1937.

41 Anthony, Edward M., Jr. Test frames for structures with
    up in modern American English. University of Michigan,
    1954.

42 Antonsen, Elmer H. The investigation of i-mutation in
    the Germanic languages. University of Illinois, 1961.

43 Applegate, Joseph R. Shilha: A descriptive grammar with
    vocabulary and texts. University of Pennsylvania, 1955.

44 Apte, Mahadeo L. A sketch of Marathi transformational
    grammar. University of Wisconsin, 1962.

45 Archer, Jerome W. Latin loan-words in early Middle
    English. Northwestern University, 1942.

46 Arndt, Walter W. Germanic dialect evolution in lexico-
    statistic time perspective. University of North Caro-
    lina, 1956.

47 Arndt, William F. The participle in Polybius and in
    Saint Paul. Washington University at St. Louis, 1935.

48 Arnold, David B. Linguistic variation in a New England
    community. Harvard University, 1962.

49 Arnold, Frederic K. The use of glide-sounds in consonant
    groups in the Romance languages. Harvard University, 1937.

50 Arnold, Richard E. A study of the Latinity of Narratio
    restaurationis abbatiae Sancti Martini Tornascensis by
    Hermann of Tournai. St. Louis University, 1936.

51 Aron, Albert W. Die 'progressiven' Formen im Mittelhoch-
    deutschen und Frühneuhochdeutschen. New York University,
    1913.

52 Aronson, Howard I. Morphophonemic patterns of the Bul-
    garian inflection. Indiana University, 1961.

53 Arthur, Ann R. The Icelandic language as described by
    Runolfur Jonsson in his Grammaticae Islandicae Rudimenta
    (1651). University of North Carolina at Chapel Hill, 1964.

54 Arts, Sister Mary R. The syntax of the Confessions of
    Saint Augustine. Catholic University of America, 1927.

55 Aston, Katharine O. A semantic study of Gothic and Old
    Icelandic words for oral expression. Bryn Mawr College,
    1958.

56 Atai, Parvin. A contrastive study of English and Persian
    question signals. University of Michigan, 1964.

57 Atkinson, Dorothy F. A study of the punctuation of
    Spenser's Faerie Queene. University of Washington, 1931.

58 Austerlitz, Robert P. The metrical structure of Ob-Ugric
    folk-poetry. Columbia University, 1955.

59 Austin, William M. The prothetic vowel in Greek. Prince-
    ton University, 1938.

60 Avis, Walter S. The mid-back vowels in the English of the
    Eastern United States: A detailed investigation of re-
    gional and social differences in phonic characteristics
    and in phonemic organization. University of Michigan,
    1956.

61 Axelrod, Joseph. A phonemic analysis of the speech of
    Jacques Peletier (1517-1582) with a facsimile of his
    Dialogue de l'ortografe. University of Chicago, 1945.

62 Babcock, Alfred R. The position of the copula and of the
    colorless ancillary verbs in Greek. Harvard University,
    1953.

63 Bach, Emmon W. Patterns of syntax in Hoelderlin's poems.
    University of Chicago, 1959.

64 Bachmann, Ann O. An etymological and partial syntactical
    analysis of the Rimado de Palacio of Pero López de Ayala.
    Florida State University, 1958.

65 Baepler, Frederick A. The particles inûma and kî in the
    Amarna tablets. Johns Hopkins University, 1943.

66 Baerg, Marjorie K.L. Gnadenau Low German: A dialect of
    Marion County, Kansas. University of Chicago, 1961.

67 Bagan, Rev. Philip V. The syntax of the letters of Pope
    Gelasius I. Catholic University of America, 1945.

68 Bailey, Beryl L. Jamaican Creole syntax: A transforma-
    tional approach. Columbia University, 1964.

69 Bailey, Don C. The Rakuyoshu and its place in the history
    of dictionaries in Japan. University of Michigan, 1960.

70 Baird, Herbert L., Jr. Un analisis lingüístico y filo-
    lógico de El Cuento Muy Fermoso Del Emperador Otas de
    Roma. University of Chicago, 1956.

71 Baker, Howard G. The contribution of John Wallis to the
    methods and materials of English grammar. University of
    Michigan, 1938.

72 Baker, Robert L. The Dvina documents of the fifteenth
    century: Establishment of text, translation, and pre-
    liminary grammatical analysis. University of Michigan,
    1962.

73 Baker, William E. The syntax of English poetry. Univer-
    sity of California at Berkeley, 1964.

74 Ball, George H. A study of the syntax of Le moyen de
    parvenir. University of California, 1939.

75 Bambas, Rudolph C. The verb in Samuel Daniel's The
    Collection of the History of England. Northwestern Uni-
    versity, 1941.

76 Barker, Glenn W. A critical evaluation of the lexical
    and linguistic data advanced by E.J. Goodspeed and sup-
    ported by C.L. Mitton in a proposed solution to the
    problem of the authorship and date of Ephesians. Harvard
    University, 1962.

77 Barker, Phillip. The Klamath language. University of
    California at Berkeley, 1959.

78 Barnhill, Viron L. Poetic context in the collected poems
    (1909-1935) of T.S. Eliot: A linguistic investigation of
    poetic context. University of Michigan, 1960.

79 Barrett, Carol E. A graphemic analysis of English nominal
    complexes. University of Texas, 1963.

80 Barrett, Ralph P., Jr. Some grammatical characteristics
    of aphasic speech. University of Michigan, 1961.

81 Barrett, William R. Problems of vocalic alternation in
    Old Icelandic nasal and liquid suffixes. University of
    North Carolina, 1948.

82   Barritt, Carlyle W.   The order classes of modifiers in
     English.   University of Virginia, 1952.

83   Barrutia, Richard.   Linguistic theory of language learn-
     ing as related to machine teaching.   University of Texas,
     1964.

84   Barry, Sister Mary F.   The vocabulary of the moral-
     ascetical works of Saint Ambrose: A study in Latin lexi-
     cography.   Catholic University of America, 1926.

85   Basilius, Harold A.   A phonology of the Alsfeld Passion
     Play as determined by the rimes.   University of Ohio,
     1935.

86   Bassett, Edward L.   De Metaphonia Latina.   Harvard Uni-
     versity, 1942.

87   Bates, Arthur S.   A linguistic study of Ly romans de
     vraye amour.   Cornell University, 1940.

88   Baumann, Elda O.   German surnames of Potosi, Wisconsin.
     University of Wisconsin, 1939.

89   Bayliss, Betty.   Sebastian de Covarrubias' Supplemento
     al Tesoro de la lengua castellana: A critical edition of
     selections from the original manuscript.   University of
     Illinois, 1959.

90   Bays, Robert A.   The semantic development of tenses in
     Spanish.   Yale University, 1958.

91   Beall, Florence G.   Concord of number in modern English
     with special reference to the indefinites.   University
     of Michigan, 1933.

92   Beardsley, Wilfred A.   Infinitive constructions in Old
     Spanish.   Columbia University, 1917.

93   Beberfall, Lester.   A history of the partitive indefinite
     construction in the Spanish language.   University of
     Michigan, 1952.

94   Bechtel, George.   Hittite verbs in -sk-: A semantic study.
     Yale University, 1934.

95   Becker, Valerie.   A transfer grammar of the verb struc-
     tures of modern Literary Arabic and Lebanese Colloquial
     Arabic.   Yale University, 1964.

96   Beebe, John F. Hypotaxis in contemporary standard
     Russian. Harvard University, 1958.

97   Beegle, Dewey W. Proper names in the Dead Sea Isaiah
     scroll (DSIa), with a detailed examination of the use of
     the vowel letters waw and yod. Johns Hopkins University,
     1953.

98   Beeler, Madison S. The phonology of Venetic. Harvard
     University, 1936.

99   Belasco, Simon. The phonetic basis of French rime: An
     articulatory, acoustic, auditory study of rime preference.
     University of Pennsylvania, 1953.

100 Bell, Edward A., Jr. The emergence of nasal vowel pho-
     nemes in French. University of Texas, 1962.

101 Bell, Elizabeth S. A phonetic approach to the relative
     intelligibility and error responses among initial con-
     sonants and consonantal clusters. Ohio State University,
     1959.

102 Belson, Joel J. The names in The Faerie Queene. Columbia
     University, 1964.

103 Bender, Byron W. A linguistic analysis of the place-
     names of the Marshall Islands. Indiana University, 1963.

104 Benedict, Paul K. Kinship in Southeastern Asia. Harvard
     University, 1941.

105 Benedict, Warren C. Urartian phonology and morphology.
     University of Michigan, 1958.

106 Benediktsson, Hreinn. The vowel system of Old Icelandic:
     Its structure and development. Harvard University, 1958.

107 Benham, Allen R. The expression of result in Old English
     prose. Yale University, 1905.

108 Bennett, Clifford A. The Latin of the Roman breviary
     hymns. University of Pittsburgh, 1942.

109 Bennett, Emmett L., Jr. The Minoan linear script from
     Pylos. University of Cincinnati, 1947.

110 Bennett, Jacob. A linguistic study of The Castle of
     Perseverance. Boston University, 1960.

111   Benson, Albert E. Pronominal ellipses in Layamon, Orm,
      and Chaucer. Harvard University, 1900.

112   Benson, Morton. The development of predicate adjective
      usage in Russian literary prose from Pushkin on. Uni-
      versity of Pennsylvania, 1954.

113   Bentley, Harold Woodmansee. A dictionary of Spanish
      terms in English, with special reference to the American
      Southwest. Columbia University, 1932.

114   Berberi, Dilaver. Phonological and morphological adap-
      tation of Turkish loanwords in contemporary Albanian
      Geg dialect of Kruja: A synchronic analysis. Indiana
      University, 1964.

115   Berger, Marshall D. The American English pronunciation
      of Russian immigrants. Columbia University, 1951.

116   Berko, Jean. The child's learning of English morphology.
      Radcliffe College, 1958.

117   Berkooz, Moshé. Orthography and phonology of the Nuzi
      dialect of Akkadian. University of Pennsylvania, 1936.

118   Bernards, Voldemars T. Laryngeal phonemes in Indo-
      European phonology. Columbia University, 1959.

119   Bernlohr, Fred A. A study of the sixty less common
      verbs of 'saying' in Plautus. University of Pennsyl-
      vania, 1940.

120   Bevans, Caleb A. The Old French vocabulary of Champagne:
      A descriptive study based on localized and dated docu-
      ments. University of Chicago, 1939.

121   Beym, Richard. The linguistic category of emphasis in
      colloquial Spanish. University of Illinois, 1952.

122   Bhatia, Rishi G. A Gypsy grammar. University of Penn-
      sylvania, 1963.

123   Bidwell, Charles E. A structural analysis of Uzbek.
      University of Pennsylvania, 1954.

124   Bieter, Rev. Fredric. The syntax of the cases and prepo-
      sitions in Cassiodorus' Historia tripertita. Catholic
      University of America, 1938.

125 Biggs, Bruce G. The structure of Maori. Indiana University, 1957.

126 Bird, Donald A. The pronunciation of Michael Drayton. University of Wisconsin, 1950.

127 Bishai, Wilson B. The Coptic influence on Egyptian Arabic. Johns Hopkins University, 1959.

128 Blackwelder, Boyce W. The casual use of prepositions in the Greek New Testament. Northern Baptist Theological Seminary, 1953.

129 Blair, Robert W. Yucatec Maya noun and verb morphosyntax. Indiana University, 1964.

130 Blaisdell, Foster W., Jr. The preposition-adverbs in the oldest Icelandic prose manuscripts. University of California at Berkeley, 1956.

131 Blanchard, Homer D. German organ-building terminology. University of Ohio, 1940.

132 Blansitt, Edward L., Jr. The verb phrase in Spanish: Classes and relations. University of Texas, 1963.

133 Blattner, Ann H. An experimental study of the testing of pronunciation. University of Iowa, 1948.

134 Blau, Bernard. The Indo-European suffix -eno-, -ono-, -no- in the Germanic past participle of strong verbs. New York University, 1949.

135 Blaylock, William C. Studies in possible Osco-Umbrian influence on Hispano-Romance phonology. University of California at Berkeley, 1964.

136 Blenner-Hassett, Roland. A study of the place-names in Lawman's Brut. Harvard University, 1940.

137 Bloch, Bernard. The treatment of Middle English final and preconsonantal r in the present-day speech of New England. Brown University, 1935.

138 Bloodworth, Bertha E. Florida place-names. University of Florida, 1959.

139 Bodle, Alice J. Legal terminology in New Testament Greek. Ohio State University, 1958.

140   Bodman, Nicholas C. A linguistic study of the <u>Shih ming</u>:
      Initials and consonant clusters. Yale University, 1950.

141   Boezinger, Bruno. Das historische Präsens in der älteren
      deutschen Sprache. Stanford University, 1912.

142   Bogan, Sister M. Inez. The vocabulary and style of the
      soliloquies and dialogues of St. Augustine. Catholic
      University of America, 1935.

143   Bond, George D. The factors governing the pronunciation
      of Chaucer's final -<u>e</u>. University of Michigan, 1947.

144   Bonhard, Florence M. A critical study of the archaisms
      in the vocabulary of Villehardouin. University of
      Southern California, 1947.

145   Boone, Lalia P. The language of the oil field. Uni-
      versity of Florida, 1951.

146   Bordie, John G. A descriptive Sindhi phonology. Uni-
      versity of Texas, 1958.

147   Borkowski, Casimir G. Kernel sentences of Polish and
      their transformations. University of Pennsylvania, 1958.

148   Bormanshinov, Arash. The Illyrian movement as reflected
      in the Serbo-Croatian literature and language. Univer-
      sity of Pennsylvania, 1958.

149   Bosco, Paul F. The phonology of the dialect of Vasto.
      Harvard University, 1943.

150   Boswell, Richard E. A semantic theory of French grammar
      and its application to the preposition before infinitive.
      Yale University, 1964.

151   Boudreau, Richard P. Expressions of atmospheric pre-
      cipitation and their distribution in the Italian dia-
      lects. Princeton University, 1953.

152   Bowdre, Paul H., Jr. A study of eye dialect. Univer-
      sity of Florida, 1964.

153   Bowen, Jean D. The Spanish of San Antoñito, New Mexico.
      University of New Mexico, 1952.

154   Bowling, Andrew C. A syntactical examination of clause
      function in late-Egyptian narrative. Brandeis Univer-
      sity, 1962.

155 Bowman, Elizabeth. The minor and fragmentary sentences
     in a corpus of spoken English. University of Chicago,
     1963.

156 Boyd, Natasha D. Graphics as a tool in communicating
     certain formulations in general semantics. University
     of Denver, 1953.

157 Boyd, Robert H. The Arabic text of I Corinthians in
     Studia Sinaitica No. II: A comparative linguistic and
     critical study. Princeton University, 1942.

158 Boyd-Bowman, Peter M. A linguistic study of the Spanish
     of Guanajuato, Mexico. Harvard University, 1950.

159 Brandt, Elisabeth H.P. A study of invariance under
     transformation in a German-English translation. Univer-
     sity of Denver, 1960.

160 Brazzel, Sister M. Kathleen. The clausulae in the works
     of St. Gregory the Great. Catholic University of
     America, 1940.

161 Brekke, Arne. Holt as an appellative and a farm-name
     element in Icelandic. University of Chicago, 1964.

162 Bremner, Ellen L. A glossary of sea terms in Old Vene-
     tian portolani. University of Illinois, 1961.

163 Brend, Ruth M. A tagmemic analysis of Mexican Spanish
     clauses. University of Michigan, 1964.

164 Brengelman, Frederick H. The native American English
     spoken in the Puget Sound area. University of Washing-
     ton, 1957.

165 Brennan, Sister M. Josephine. The clausulae in the
     sermons of Saint Augustine. Catholic University of
     America, 1947.

166 Brenninger, Ralph A. A study of the Fugger financial
     vocabulary, 1494-1525. University of California at
     Berkeley, 1944.

167 Bridgman, Richard. The stylization of vernacular ele-
     ments in American fiction, 1880-1925. University of
     California at Berkeley, 1961.

168 Brière, Eugène J. On defining a hierarchy of difficulty
     of learning phonological categories. University of
     Washington, 1964.

169 Bright, William O. A grammar of the Karok language.
     University of California at Berkeley, 1955.

170 Brister, Zeb L. An investigation of the grammatical
     construction in the Book of Revelation. Southwestern
     Baptist Theological Seminary, 1953.

171 Bronstein, Arthur J. A study of predominant dialect
     variations of standard speech in the United States dur-
     ing the first half of the nineteenth century. New York
     University, 1949.

172 Brooks, Maria Z. An acoustic analysis of nasal vowels
     in contemporary standard Polish. University of Michigan,
     1963.

173 Brosman, Margaret C. The verbal concept of motion in
     Old Spanish. University of North Carolina, 1956.

174 Brosman, Paul W., Jr. The verbal concept of motion in
     Old French. University of North Carolina, 1956.

175 Brotherton, Blanche E.M. The vocabulary of intrigue in
     Roman comedy. University of Chicago, 1921.

176 Brown, Anita Dolores. A linguistic analysis of St.
     Paul's Epistle to the Romans and prologues to the
     Epistles in MS I.1.2 of the library of the Escorial.
     University of Wisconsin, 1957.

177 Brown, Augustus F. The derivation of English adjectives
     ending -ful. University of Pennsylvania, 1958.

178 Brown, Carleton F. A study of the English grammar
     schools before the reformation. Harvard University,
     1903.

179 Brown, Faith S. Intonation in German interrogative sen-
     tences. Northwestern University, 1951.

180 Brown, George O. Syllabification and accent in Paradise
     Lost. Johns Hopkins University, 1901.

181   Brown, James M.   From Ancient Thai to modern dialects:
      A theory.   Cornell University, 1962.

182   Brown, Milton P.   A linguistic analysis of the longer
      Ignatian Corpus to establish criteria of authenticity.
      Duke University, 1959.

183   Brown, Sister M. Vincentia.   The syntax of the prepo-
      sitions in the works of St. Hilary.   Catholic Univer-
      sity of America, 1935.

184   Brown, Roger L.   Some sources and aspects of Wilhelm von
      Humboldt's conception of linguistic relativity.   Uni-
      versity of Illinois, 1964.

185   Brown, William H., Jr.   A descriptive syntax of King
      Alfred's Pastoral Care.   University of Michigan, 1963.

186   Bruns, Sister M. Magdalita.   The language of the Roman
      missal.   St. Louis University, 1947.

187   Bryan, William F.   Studies in the dialects of the Kentish
      charters of the Old English period.   University of
      Chicago, 1913.

188   Bryant, Margaret M.   English in the law courts: The part
      that articles, prepositions and conjunctions play in
      legal decisions.   Columbia University, 1930.

189   Buchanan, Charles D.   Substantivized adjectives in Old
      Norse.   Cornell University, 1932.

190   Buchner, Margaret L.   A study of the vocabulary of Jean-
      Jacques Rousseau.   Johns Hopkins University, 1936.

191   Buck, Frederick H.   Comparative study of post-positions
      in Mongolian dialects and the written language.   Harvard
      University, 1953.

192   Buckalew, Ronald E.   A generative grammar of Gothic mor-
      phology.   University of Illinois, 1964.

193   Bucklin, Lincoln B.   Liturgical influence on popular
      Spanish.   Johns Hopkins University, 1952.

194   Buffington, Albert F.   A grammatical and linguistic study
      of Pennsylvania German.   Harvard University, 1937.

195   Bulatkin, Eleanor W. The expression of the concept
      'nuance' in Spanish, Italian, and French. Johns Hopkins
      University, 1952.

196   Bulos, Afif A. The structure of the triliteral verb in
      modern literary Arabic: A comparative analysis of gram-
      matical concepts and processes. Harvard University,
      1961.

197   Burch, J. Charles H. A combined lexicon and concordance
      of the English works of John Gower, A-C inclusive. Duke
      University, 1933.

198   Burkett, Eva M. A study of American dictionaries of the
      English language before 1861. George Peabody College
      for Teachers, 1936.

199   Burkhart, Russell S. The syntax of place in Old English
      prose. University of Pittsburgh, 1935.

200   Burnham, Josephine M. Concessive constructions in Old
      English prose. Yale University, 1910.

201   Burtness, Paul S. A language study of the Awntyrs off
      Arthure at the Terne Wathelyn. University of Chicago,
      1953.

202   Bush, Frederic W. A grammar of the Hurrian language.
      Brandeis University, 1964.

203   Butler, Roy F. Index verborum comicorum Romanorum
      fragmentorum. University of Ohio, 1942.

204   Butler, Thomas J. The Serbian literary language contro-
      versy: 1814-1817. Harvard University, 1963.

205   Butros, Albert J. English loanwords in the Colloquial
      Arabic of Palestine (1917-1948) and Jordan (1948-1962).
      Columbia University, 1963.

206   Bynum, David E. A taxonomy of oral narrative song: The
      isolation and description of invariables in Serbo-
      Croatian tradition. Harvard University, 1964.

207   Byrne, Sister St. Geraldine. Shakespeare's use of the
      pronoun of address: Its significance in characterization
      and motivation. Catholic University of America, 1936.

208   Caffee, Nathaniel M.   A phonological study of the speech
      of a homogeneous group in Charlottesville, Virginia.
      University of Virginia, 1935.

209   Caldwell, Robert A.   Linguistic peculiarities of the
      Cambridge University Library Manuscript Gg4.27.   Uni-
      versity of Chicago, 1938.

210   Callaghan, Catherine A.   A grammar of the Lake Miwok
      language.   University of California at Berkeley, 1963.

211   Cameron, Jeremiah.   Multiple negation in written English.
      Michigan State University, 1957.

212   Cammack, Floyd M.   Bauan grammar.   Cornell University,
      1962.

213   Campbell, Anna L.   A study of some factors in the writ-
      ten language of a group of Texas land-grant college
      freshmen to show how the nature of the language reflects
      the socio-economic backgrounds of these students.   New
      York University, 1956.

214   Campbell, Charles B.   Concerning the pronominal antece-
      dent and the form of the accompanying relative pronoun
      in modern German prose.   University of Chicago, 1912.

215   Campbell, Ernest R.   Word studies in the Greek papyri.
      Ohio State University, 1953.

216   Campbell, Russell N.   Noun substitutes in modern Thai.
      University of Michigan, 1964.

217   Canfield, Delos L.   Spanish literature in Mexican lan-
      guages as a source for the study of Spanish pronunci-
      ation.   Columbia University, 1934.

218   Capps, Edward, III.   The compound words in Pindar.   Yale
      University, 1964.

219   Cárdenas, Daniel N.   The Spanish of Jalisco: A contri-
      bution to Spanish-American linguistic geography.   Colum-
      bia University, 1953.

220   Cardona, George.   The Indo-European thematic aorists.
      Yale University, 1960.

221   Carlson, Arthur F.   The orthography and phonology of the
      Latin papyri.   University of Michigan, 1950.

222 Carlson, Helen S. Nevada place-names: Origin and mean-
     ing. University of New Mexico, 1959.

223 Carlton, Ainsley M. A relative chronology of Old Ice-
     landic sound laws. Stanford University, 1941.

224 Carlton, Charles M. A linguistic analysis of a collec-
     tion of Late Latin documents composed in Ravenna between
     A.D. 445-700. University of Michigan, 1963.

225 Carlton, Charles R. Syntax of the Old English charters.
     University of Michigan, 1958.

226 Carr, Denzel R. Certain verb formations in modern
     Japanese. Yale University, 1937.

227 Carr, Elizabeth B. Trends in word compounding in Amer-
     ican speech. Louisiana State University, 1954.

228 Carroll, Sister M. Borromeo. The clausulae in the Con-
     fessions of St. Augustine. Catholic University of Amer-
     ica, 1940.

229 Carrow, Sister Mary A. A comparative study of the lin-
     guistic functioning of bilingual Spanish-American chil-
     dren and monolingual Anglo-American children at the
     third grade level. Northwestern University, 1955.

230 Carter, Henry H. Paleographical edition and study of
     the language of a portion of Codex Alcobacensis 200.
     University of Pennsylvania, 1937.

231 Carton, Irving S. Initial /sl/ in English. Columbia
     University, 1956.

232 Cassidy, Frederic G. The backgrounds in Old English of
     the modern English substitutes for the dative object in
     the group verb + dative object + accusative object.
     University of Michigan, 1939.

233 Castelo, Lutgarda M. Structural differences between
     English and Tagalog verbs: A study designed to improve
     the teaching of English to advanced Filipino students.
     Columbia University, 1962.

234 Causey, James Y. A cultural study of the agricultural
     terms in the works of Alfonso el Sabio. University of
     Wisconsin, 1941.

235   Caviness, George L.   Ein Beitrag zum Wortschatz des
      Pietismus.   University of Ohio, 1948.

236   Chafe, Wallace L.   Seneca morphology.   Yale University,
      1958.

237   Chaiyaratana, Chalao.   A comparative study of English
      and Thai syntax.   Indiana University, 1961.

238   Chambers, Frank M.   Uses of the subjunctive mood in the
      Romance languages.   Harvard University, 1935.

239   Chang, Kun.   The Kathinavasta.   Yale University, 1955.

240   Chapman, Kenneth G.   Icelandic-Norwegian linguistic
      relationships.   University of Wisconsin, 1957.

241   Chappel, Allen H.   Saga of Victor ok Blavus: A fifteenth
      century Icelandic Lygisaga: An English edition and trans-
      lation based chiefly on AM593b, 4to.   University of North
      Carolina at Chapel Hill, 1963.

242   Chatham, James R.   A syntactical study of the indirect
      interrogatives in Old Spanish.   Florida State University,
      1960.

243   Chatman, Seymour B.   Structural and lexical distributions
      of function words with substantives in the Paston Letters
      (1440-1460).   University of Michigan, 1956.

244   Chatterjee, Suhas.   A study of the relationship between
      written and colloquial Bengali.   Hartford Seminary
      Foundation, 1962.

245   Chavarria-Aguilar, Oscar L.   A grammar of Pashto.   Uni-
      versity of Pennsylvania, 1952.

246   Cheek, John H., Jr.   A distinctive feature phonematic
      analysis of Lower Sorbian.   Harvard University, 1959.

247   Chew, John J., Jr.   A transformational analysis of modern
      colloquial Japanese.   Yale University, 1961.

248   Chisholm, Francis P.   Grammatical structure in linguistic
      behavior: An introduction to the general study of lan-
      guage.   Syracuse University, 1944.

249   Chisholm, William S.   Sentence patterns in The Sound and
      the Fury.   University of Michigan, 1964.

250   Chomsky, Avram Noam.   Transformational analysis.   University of Pennsylvania, 1955.

251   Chou, Kuo-ping.   The uses of the function-word at in present-day standard English.   University of Michigan, 1952.

252   Chude, Fannie.   Hapax legomena: A linguistic study of words occurring once.   Radcliffe College, 1954.

253   Chung, Kei Won.   The origins of the Korean alphabet. Princeton University, 1938.

254   Church, Henry W.   The compound past tenses, active and passive, in Middle High German as represented by Heinrich von Veldeke, Gottfried von Strassburg, and Wolfram von Eschenbach.   University of Michigan, 1915.

255   Ciani, Amerigo.   Friulian vowels, with special reference to literary Friulian.   University of California at Berkeley, 1949.

256   Cizevska, Tanja.   The vocabulary of the Igor' tale compared with other Old Russian texts.   Radcliffe College, 1955.

257   Clardy, Catherine J.   Pampango phonology.   University of Texas, 1958.

258   Clark, John W.   The authorship of Sir Gawain and the Green Knight, Pearl, Cleanness, Patience, and Erkenwald in light of the vocabulary.   University of Minnesota, 1941.

259   Clark, Richard C.   The present state of Dutch dialect studies in the Netherlands and Belgium.   University of Pennsylvania, 1954.

260   Clark, Warren J.   An analytical study of the influence of English orthography on foreign accent.   University of Denver, 1954.

261   Clay, Dorothy M.   A formal analysis of the vocabularies of Aeschylus, Sophocles, and Euripides.   University of Minnesota, 1957.

262   Cleaves, Francis W.   A Sino-Mongolian inscription of 1362.   Harvard University, 1942.

263   Clemens, George B.   A tentative Portuguese dictionary
      of dated first occurrences to the year 1350.   University
      of Pennsylvania, 1949.

264   Clemons, Elinor D.   A metrical analysis of the Old Eng-
      lish poem Exodus.   University of Texas, 1961.

265   Clevy, Lloyd S.   A linguistic study of the journals of
      the Coronado expedition.   University of Colorado, 1958.

266   Clifton, Ernest S.   A study of consonantal dissimilation
      in English.   Louisiana State University, 1940.

267   Closs, Olwen E.E.   A grammar of Alfred's Orosius.   Uni-
      versity of California at Berkeley, 1964.

268   Cobb, George W.   The subjunctive mood in Old English
      poetry.   Johns Hopkins University, 1937.

269   Colby, Lore M.   Zinacantan Tzotzil sound and word struc-
      ture.   Harvard University, 1964.

270   Coleman, Evelyn S.   Die Lehnbildungen in Notker Labeos
      Übersetzung De Consolatione Philosophiae von A.M.S.
      Boetius.   Harvard University, 1963.

271   Collins, Henry E.   A phonology of the dialect of South-
      ern Warwickshire.   Yale University, 1964.

272   Coltharp, Mary L.   The influence of English on the 'lan-
      guage' of the Tirilones.   University of Texas, 1964.

273   Conant, Carlos E.   The pepet law in Philippine languages.
      University of Chicago, 1911.

274   Conley, John A.   Four studies in Aureate terms.   Stan-
      ford University, 1956.

275   Connell, Chester C.   The closing of atonic vowels in the
      Romance languages.   Harvard University, 1936.

276   Conner, Jack E.   A history of double vowels in English
      spelling.   Stanford University, 1953.

277   Conrad, Carl W.   From epic to lyric: A study in the his-
      tory of traditional word-order in Greek and Latin poetry.
      Harvard University, 1964.

278   Conrad, Joseph L.   Study of the Germanic languages in the Soviet Union (1934-1960).   University of Texas, 1961.

279   Conroy, Kenneth C.   A glossary of John Trevisa's translation of the De Regímine Principum of Aegidius Romanus. University of Washington, 1964.

280   Constantino, Ernesto A.   A generative grammar of a dialect of Ilocano.   Indiana University, 1959.

281   Contreras, Heles.   The phonological system of a bilingual child.   Indiana University, 1961.

282   Conway, Sister M. Ann C.   Order classes of adjectives in Spanish.   University of Texas, 1964.

283   Conwell, Marilyn J.   Lafayette French phonology: A descriptive, comparative, and historical study of a Louisiana French dialect.   University of Pennsylvania, 1961.

284   Cook, Mary J.   Phonetic and phonemic properties of stress in English.   University of Texas, 1961.

285   Cooper, Louis.   A linguistic study of the 'Liber regum' of the Cronicón villarense.   University of Chicago, 1952.

286   Cooper, Paul J.   The language of the Forum judicum. Columbia University, 1953.

287   Copeland, Robert M.   The language of Herz's Esther: A study in Judeo-German dialectology.   Harvard University, 1952.

288   Cornelius, Paul E.   Languages in seventeenth- and early eighteenth-century imaginary voyages.   Columbia University, 1962.

289   Cornyn, William S.   Outline of Burmese grammar.   Yale University, 1944.

290   Corré, Alan D.   The structure of Tamil.   University of Pennsylvania, 1962.

291   Cosper, Russell.   The English question patterns from 1100 to 1600.   University of Michigan, 1948.

292   Cotton, Jack C.   A study of certain phoniatric resonance phenomena.   University of Ohio, 1936.

293 Cottrell, Alice B. A group test for ascertaining abil-
     ity in phonetic analysis among college freshmen. Stan-
     ford University, 1958.

294 Coughanowr, Euphrosyne N. The verbal categories in the
     Greek of the synoptic gospels. University of Illinois,
     1955.

295 Covey, Delvin L. Psychological vocabulary in Roman
     poetry. University of Illinois, 1952.

296 Cowan, J Milton. Pitch, intensity and rhythmic move-
     ments in American dramatic speech. University of Iowa,
     1936.

297 Cowan, William G. A reconstruction of Proto-Colloquial
     Arabic. Cornell University, 1960.

298 Cowgill, Warren C. The Indo-European long-vowel pret-
     erits. Yale University, 1957.

299 Cowles, Ella N. A vocabulary of American Spanish based
     on glossaries appended to literary works. University
     of Michigan, 1952.

300 Cox, Willa C. A study of English prepositions. George
     Peabody College for Teachers, 1941.

301 Coxe, Malcolm S. A history of the spelling of English
     phonemes. Louisiana State University, 1942.

302 Coxe, Warren W. The influence of Latin on the spelling
     of English words. Ohio State University, 1923.

303 Crabb, David M. A comparative study of word order in
     Old Spanish and Old French prose works. Catholic Uni-
     versity, 1955.

304 Cramer, Richard W. The legal language of the Pauline
     epistles. Dallas Theological Seminary and Dallas School
     of Theology, 1952.

305 Crawford, Fredrick S., Jr. Quo modo Graeci vocales e
     et o designaverint. Harvard University, 1938.

306 Crawford, John C. Pike's tagmemic model applied to
     Totontepec Mixe phonology. University of Michigan, 1960.

307 Crawford, Vaughn E. Terminology of the leather industry
     in late Sumerian times. Yale University, 1948.

308   Creore, Alvin E. The language of Du Bartas. Johns
      Hopkins University, 1939.

309   Criswell, Elijah H. Lewis and Clark: Linguistic pio-
      neers. University of Missouri, 1957.

310   Croft, Kenneth. Matlapa and Classical Nahuatl: With
      comparative notes on the two dialects. Indiana Univer-
      sity, 1953.

311   Crossgrove, William C. Vowel quantity in Proto-Germanic.
      University of Texas, 1962.

312   Crotty, John M. The language in the plays of John
      Marston. University of Notre Dame, 1956.

313   Crowell, Thomas L., Jr. A study of the verb get.
      Columbia University, 1956.

314   Crowley, Cornelius J. Persisting Latinisms in El poema
      de mio Cid and other selected Old Spanish literary works.
      New York University, 1951.

315   Crump, James I., Jr. Some problems in the language of
      the Shīn-Bian Wuu-Day Shyy Pyng-Huah. Yale University,
      1950.

316   Cryesky, Ralph H. A semantic study of verbs of thinking
      in the Romance languages. Harvard University, 1953.

317   Cummings, Francis J. Caesar's vocabulary as reflected
      in French. University of Pennsylvania, 1933.

318   Cunningham, Maurice P. The singular and plural of sub-
      stantives in Latin poetic diction. University of Cali-
      fornia, 1941.

319   Curl, Thelma D. Word building through the use of Greek
      and Latin roots and affixes. Columbia University, 1963.

320   Curran, Leo C. Studies in the language of Propertius I.
      Yale University, 1961.

321   Curry, Victor B. The nature and use of the ἵνα clause
      in the New Testament. Southern Baptist Theological
      Seminary, 1949.

322   Curtis, Jay L. The vocabulary of medical Craftas in the
      Old English Leechbook of Bald. University of North
      Carolina, 1946.

323   Curtis, John J.   An application of the syntax of Hebrew
      verbs to the writings of Amos.   Southern Baptist Theo-
      logical Seminary, 1949.

324   Curtis, Roy G.   An investigation of some of the struc-
      tures of independent utterances in modern American Eng-
      lish.   University of Michigan, 1948.

325   Dahood, Mitchell J.   Canaanite-Phoenician influence in
      Qoheleth.   Johns Hopkins University, 1951.

326   Dailey, Virginia L.   A metrical analysis of the Old Eng-
      lish poem Juliana.   University of Texas, 1963.

327   Daly, Charles B.   General semantics and the rule of
      stare decisis as regards the Supreme Court of the United
      States since 1937.   New York University, 1953.

328   Daniel, John F.   Prolegomena to the Cypro-Minoan script.
      University of Pennsylvania, 1941.

329   Danowitz, Edward F.   A guide to the teaching of Russian
      military terminology to U.S. Marine Corps personnel.
      University of Pennsylvania, 1956.

330   D'Arms, Edward F.   Chapters on the style of the Roman
      elegy: The verb.   Princeton University, 1936.

331   Dato, Daniel P.   A historical phonology of Castilian.
      Cornell University, 1959.

332   Daugman, Joseph.   Long vowel augments in Sanskrit and
      Greek aorists.   University of Wisconsin, 1952.

333   Davis, Alva L.   A word atlas of the Great Lakes region.
      University of Michigan, 1949.

334   Davis, George Tobey.   A study in Latin prosody: Short
      final vowel before initial consonant groups composed of
      stop and liquid.   University of Pennsylvania, 1959.

335   Davis, Irvine E.   Grammatical structure of Santa Ana
      Keresan.   University of New Mexico, 1960.

336   Davis, Jack E.   Estudio lexicográfico de El Periquillo
      Sarniento.   Tulane University, 1956.

337   Davis, John C.   The use of the subjunctive and the con-
      ditional in the Perlesvaus.   University of Chicago, 1937.

338   Davis, Richard M. An experimental approach to effective
      industrial communications. University of Michigan, 1962.

339   Dawson, Clayton L. The derivational suffixes of the
      Russian substantive: A synchronic study. Harvard Uni-
      versity, 1954.

340   Dearden, E. Jeannette. Dialect areas of the South
      Atlantic states as determined by variations in vocabu-
      lary. Brown University, 1943.

341   DeCamp, David. The pronunciation of English in San
      Francisco. University of California at Berkeley, 1954.

342   Deferrari, Roy J. Lucian's Atticism, the morphology of
      the verb. Princeton University, 1915.

343   DeForest, John B. Old French borrowed words in the Old
      Spanish of the twelfth and thirteenth centuries, with
      special reference to the Cid, Berceo's poems, the
      Alexandre and Fernán González. Yale University, 1915.

344   deGorog, Ralph P. The Scandinavian element in French
      and Norman. Columbia University, 1954.

345   Deitz, Patricia. The relative frequency of correlations
      and oppositions phonologiques in modern French. Uni-
      versity of Iowa, 1952.

346   DeLand, Graydon S. An etymological vocabulary to the
      books of Exodus and Leviticus of the General estoria
      of Alfonso el Sabio. University of Wisconsin, 1936.

347   Delattre, Pierre C. La durée des e d'un français:
      Etude de phonétique experimentale. University of
      Michigan, 1937.

348   DeMent, Russell D. An etymological lexicon of El Poema
      de Alfonso Onceno. University of North Carolina, 1961.

349   DeMott, Benjamin H. A study of constructed languages
      in England with special reference to their relations
      with science and attitudes toward literary style, 1605-
      1686. Harvard University, 1953.

350   Demoz, Abraham. Meaning of some derived verbal stems of
      Amharic. University of California at Los Angeles, 1964.

351   Denlinger, Paul B. Studies in Middle Chinese. Univer-
      sity of Washington, 1962.

352   Denner, Karl. The dative of accompaniment in Old English poetry. Johns Hopkins University, 1951.

353   Dennis, William D.   Special uses of the imperfect subjunctive in the works of the French chroniclers of the fifteenth century. Boston University, 1960.

354   Derbyshire, William W.   Verbal homonymy in Russian. University of Pennsylvania, 1964.

355   DeRosa, Michelangelo.   The suffixes -arius, um and -aticus, um in the medieval Latin documents of Italy. Columbia University, 1953.

356   Deutsch, Rosamund E.   The pattern of sound in Lucretius. Bryn Mawr College, 1937.

357   DeVault, Joseph J.   A study of early Hebrew personal names. Johns Hopkins University, 1956.

358   DiBlasi, Sebastiano.   Principles of definition in contemporary monolingual Italian lexicography. University of Pennsylvania, 1964.

359   Dickenson, Fredrick W.A.   The use of the optative mood in the works of St. John Chrysostom. Catholic University of America, 1926.

360   Dimock, George E., Jr.   The use of the participles in Lysias. Yale University, 1949.

361   Dingwall, William O.   Diaglossic grammar. Georgetown University, 1964.

362   Dinneen, David A.   A left to right generative grammar of French. Harvard University, 1963.

363   Dinneen, Sister Lucilla.   Titles of address in Christian Greek epistolography to 527 A.D.   Catholic University of America, 1929.

364   Di Pietro, Robert J.   The structural description of an Alcamese Sicilian dialect in America. Cornell University, 1960.

365   Dirks, Hellmut G.   Development of aspects in German. Northwestern University, 1934.

366   Diver, William G.   The relation of Latin to Oscan-Umbrian. Columbia University, 1953.

367   Domincovitch, Ruth. Portuguese orthography to 1500.
      University of Pennsylvania, 1947.

368   Doty, Edith A. A glossary of 'Filipinismos' in the
      Spanish language found in Philippine publications of the
      period 1890-1920. University of Michigan, 1958.

369   Douglass, Ralph T. The evolution of Spanish orthography
      from 1475-1726. University of Pennsylvania, 1964.

370   Downer, James W. Features of New England rustic pronun-
      ciation in James Russell Lowell's Biglow Papers. Uni-
      versity of Michigan, 1958.

371   Doyle, Bro. C. Joseph. The syntax of the prepositions
      ab, de, and ex in the commentary on Virgil attributed
      to Servius. Fordham University, 1941.

372   Draffkorn, Anne E. Hurrians and Hurrian at Alalaḫ: An
      ethno-linguistic analysis. University of Pennsylvania,
      1959.

373   Dreher, John J. A comparison of native and acquired
      language intonation. University of Michigan, 1951.

374   Dressler, Rev. Hermigild. The usage of aokew and its
      cognates in Greek documents to 100 A.D. Catholic Uni-
      versity of America, 1948.

375   Droege, Geart B. Personal names contained in place
      names: Germanic personal names in Middle Dutch place
      names of Bergen (French Flanders), 1389-1400. North-
      western University, 1964.

376   Druham, Rev. David R. The syntax of Bede's Historia
      ecclesiastica. Catholic University of America, 1939.

377   DuBrau, Richard T. The Strasbourg Oaths: The Romance
      oaths in their relation to the Frankish loyalty oaths
      and in their linguistic position with respect to Vulgar
      Latin and the Romance vernacular. Stanford University,
      1952.

378   Ducibella, Joseph W. The phonology of the Sicilian
      dialects. Catholic University of America, 1936.

379   Duckert, Audrey R. The dialect of Germania Inferior:
      Phonology. Radcliffe College, 1959.

380 Duke, Francis J. A phonetic study of Italo-American speech in Richmond, Virginia. University of Virginia, 1938.

381 Duncan, Robert M. An etymological vocabulary of plant names in the works of Alfonso el Sabio. University of Wisconsin, 1936.

382 Dunlap, Arthur R. The vocabulary and dialect of the Middle English romances in tail-rhyme stanza. Yale University, 1934.

383 Dutton, Emily H. Studies in Greek prepositional phrases, διά, ἀπό, ἐκ, εἰς, ἐν. University of Chicago, 1913.

384 Dwyer, William F. The vocabulary of Hegesippus: A study in Latin lexicography. Catholic University of America, 1931.

385 Dyck, Henry D. Language differentation in two Low German groups in Canada. University of Pennsylvania, 1964.

386 Dyen, Isidore. The Sanskrit indeclinables of the Hindu grammarians and lexicographers. University of Pennsylvania, 1939.

387 Dykstra, Gerald. A spectrographic analysis of Spanish sibilants and its relation to Navarro's physiological phonetic descriptions. University of Michigan, 1955.

388 Eastlack, Charles L. The morphology of the verb in Portuguese. University of Texas, 1964.

389 Ebeling, Carl L. The parts of the sentence in modern Russian: A structural analysis. Harvard University, 1950.

390 Echols, John M. The numerals 1-10 in Indo-European: A study of the cardinals. University of Virginia, 1940.

391 Eddy, Frederick D. Principles governing affinity between the members of intervocalic pairs of consonants in French. University of Pennsylvania, 1951.

392 Eddy, Helen M. The French element in English. University of Iowa, 1925.

393 Edgerton, Mills F., Jr. Color terms in Transitional Latin. Princeton University, 1960.

394 Edinger, Harry G. Vocabulary and imagery in Aeschylus' Persians. Princeton University, 1961.

395 Edwards, Prior Maximilian H. A basic vocabulary of Rumanian. University of Pennsylvania, 1959.

396 Eickmann, Walter T. The semasiological development of the pronominal adverbs of motion in Old High German. New York University, 1939.

397 Eisenhardt, Catheryn T. A manual for the teaching of punctuation in the upper elementary grades, based on the research of modern linguists. New York University, 1962.

398 Ekhtiaredin, Mansour A. Emerson's poetic language: A linguistic and literary investigation. Indiana University, 1960.

399 El-Araby, Salah A.M. A taxonomy of adverbial units in contemporary American English with special emphasis on their order in post-verbal position. Columbia University, 1963.

400 El-Bettar, Abdul K.S. The linguistic concept underlying the construction of the Oxford English Course for Iraq. University of Michigan, 1962.

401 Eliason, Norman E. Vowel shortening in English. Johns Hopkins University, 1936.

402 Elfenbein, Josef H. The Tocharian verbal system. Princeton University, 1950.

403 Elkin, Celia Z. Eine semantische Untersuchung des Gotischen und andrer germanischer Dialekte im Sinnbezirk des Verstandes. Bryn Mawr College, 1954.

404 Ellenbogen, Maximilian. A study of foreign words occurring in the Hebrew and Aramaic of the Old Testament. Columbia University, 1957.

405 Ellert, Ernest E. The etymology and semantic development of words of family relationship in the Germanic languages. University of North Carolina, 1948.

406 Ellis, Herbert A. Shakespeare's punning in Love's Labours Lost. University of North Carolina at Chapel Hill, 1963.

407   Elmendorf, John von G.   An etymological dictionary of
      the Dalmatian dialect of Veglia.   University of North
      Carolina, 1952.

408   Elmore, Jefferson.   The syntax of certain Latin verbs
      of desire in the literature of the Republic.   Stanford
      University, 1901.

409   El Sayed, Dawood H.A.   A descriptive analysis of the
      part-of-speech system and the grammatical categories of
      Egyptian Colloquial Arabic.   Cornell University, 1962.

410   Elson, Benjamin F., Jr.   Sierra Popoluca morphology.
      Cornell University, 1956.

411   Elsworth, Sharlee M.   Principles of definition in mono-
      lingual French lexicography.   University of Pennsyl-
      vania, 1962.

412   Emberson, Frances G.   The vocabulary of Samuel L. Clemens
      from 1852 to 1884.   University of Missouri, 1932.

413   Emma, Ronald D.   Milton's grammar.   Duke University, 1960.

414   Engler, Leo F.   Problems in English/German contrastive
      analysis.   University of Texas, 1962.

415   English, James H.   The alternation of h and f of Old
      Spanish.   Columbia University, 1926.

416   Englund, Pearl K.   Ngbaka: Phonology and verb morphology.
      Northwestern University, 1963.

417   Ennis, Sister Mary G.   Vocabulary of the Institutiones
      of Cassiodorus: A morphological and semasiological study.
      Catholic University of America, 1937.

418   Erazmus, Edward T.   Some features of morpheme recurrence
      in Middle English syntax.   University of Michigan, 1962.

419   Ericson, Eston E.   The use of the schwa in Old English.
      Johns Hopkins University, 1928.

420   Erwin, Wallace M.   A short reference grammar of Iraqi
      Arabic.   Georgetown University, 1964.

421   Eshelman, Thomas C.   Syntaktische Studien zur Augsburger
      Urkundensprache des 13. Jahrhunderts.   University of
      Cincinnati, 1961.

422   Esper, Erwin A.   A technique for the experimental in-
      vestigation of associative interference in artificial
      linguistic material.   Ohio State University, 1923.

423   Evans, Jack.   The relationship between an awareness of
      linguistic science and attitudes toward debatable items
      of usage among teachers of English as a foreign lan-
      guage.   New York University, 1964.

424   Evans, William W., Jr.   The second-person pronoun in
      Sir Gawain and the Green Knight.   University of Florida,
      1959.

425   Everett, Paul E., Jr.   The history of nasal consonants
      and of vocalic nasalization in the Romance languages.
      Harvard University, 1939.

426   Eystone, Maxine A.   Tests and treatment of compound sub-
      stantives in Modern American English with special empha-
      sis on stress and intonation patterns.   Michigan State
      University, 1954.

427   Fairbanks, Gordon H.   Phonology and morphology of modern
      spoken West Armenian.   University of Wisconsin, 1948.

428   Falk, Lilian R.   A study of some syntactic features in
      the O.E. translation of Gregory's Dialogues.   Harvard
      University, 1963.

429   Fallis, Roy F., Jr.   The linguistic position of Old
      Saxon.   Yale University, 1951.

430   Fargo, Nancy L.   Some English affix classes.   Georgetown
      University, 1964.

431   Farley, Rodger A.   Interrogative patterns of sentence
      units in contemporary Castilian dramatic speech.   Florida
      State University, 1956.

432   Farr, James M.   Intensives and reflexives in Anglo-Saxon
      and Early Middle English.   Johns Hopkins University,
      1901.

433   Farrison, William E.   The phonology of the illiterate
      Negro dialect of Guilford County, North Carolina.   Uni-
      versity of Ohio, 1937.

434   Farzan, Massud.   A linguistic study of adverbial clauses
      in the contemporary English essay with pedagogical appli-
      cations.   University of Michigan, 1964.

435   Fassum, Ernest C. An analysis of certain characteristics
      of oral language vocabulary of junior college students.
      University of Iowa, 1942.

436   Faucett, Lawrence W. The revision of scientific lan-
      guage principles for oriental application in the teach-
      ing of English. University of Chicago, 1926.

437   Faust, Naomi F. The extent to which pivotal linguistic
      concepts are incorporated into selected English language
      textbooks of secondary schools. New York University,
      1963.

438   Fawcett, Vera E. English grammar in American public
      schools from 1890 to 1940. George Peabody College for
      Teachers, 1943.

439   Fay, Percival B. Elliptical partitive usage in affirma-
      tive clauses in French prose of the fourteenth, fifteenth,
      and sixteenth centuries. Johns Hopkins University, 1912.

440   Fee, Mary. Functional grammar and its relation to cor-
      rect English usage. University of Kansas, 1938.

441   Feinberg, Charles L. Canaanite influence on the lan-
      guage of Job. Johns Hopkins University, 1945.

442   Feldman, David M. The historical syntax of modal verb
      phrases in Spanish. Cornell University, 1963.

443   Fenn, Johnnye A. The speech of Haynesville, Louisiana,
      at three age levels. Louisiana State University, 1938.

444   Fenner, Rest, Jr. An exploratory study of some variables
      for measuring ability of students entering college with
      diversified training in French to learn to speak the
      language. Syracuse University, 1955.

445   Ferguson, Charles A. The phonology and morphology of
      standard colloquial Bengali. University of Pennsyl-
      vania, 1945.

446   Ferrell, James O. The syntax of the gerund and the
      participle in Pushkin's prose works. Columbia Univer-
      sity, 1950.

447   Ferrigno, James M. Linguistic patterns of the Iberian
      Peninsula in Sicilian and other southern Italian dia-
      lects. Boston University, 1951.

448   Fey, Richard K.H.   Neuhochdeutsche Appositionsgruppen unter besonderer Berücksichtigung der psychologischen Verhältnisse untersucht.   University of Pennsylvania, 1911.

449   Filbey, Edward J.   The supplementary participle in Herodotus.   University of Wisconsin, 1908.

450   Fillmore, Charles J.   A system for characterizing phonological theories.   University of Michigan, 1962.

451   Finder, Morris.   Descriptive English in the classroom. University of Chicago, 1960.

452   Fingeld, Thomas E.   An experimental study of the ability to select words to convey intended meaning.   University of Illinois, 1953.

453   Finn, Margaret.   A history of Latin palaeography.   Fordham University, 1950.

454   Finocchiaro, Mary B.   The Gallo-Italian dialect of Nicosia.   Columbia University, 1950.

455   Fiore, Dolores A.   Greco-Roman elements in the vocabulary of Rubén Darío.   Radcliffe College, 1958.

456   Firestone, Robert T.   The case system of modern standard German.   Indiana University, 1962.

457   Fisher, Hilda B.   A study of the speech of East Feliciana Parish, Louisiana.   Louisiana State University, 1950.

458   Fisher, Hope.   A study of sentence-stress in English poetry and prose.   University of Michigan, 1922.

459   Fisher, John C.   The application of linguistic description and oral pattern practice in remedial English composition.   University of Michigan, 1962.

460   Fishman, Peter.   The vocalism of the Messapic dialect. Harvard University, 1934.

461   Fittabile, Leo F.   An introduction, glossary, and index for An Alphabet of Tales.   Boston University, 1957.

462   Fitzgerald, Rev. William H.   The word-group honos-honestus-inhonestus in the Latin literature of the early Republic.   Fordham University, 1957.

463   Fitzmyer, Joseph A.   The syntax of imperial Aramaic
      based on the documents found in Egypt.   Johns Hopkins
      University, 1956.

464   Fives, Rev. Daniel C.   The use of the optative mood in
      the works of Theodoret, Bishop of Cyrrhus.   Catholic Uni-
      versity of America, 1937.

465   Fjelstad, Ruth N.   Archaisms in Amadís de Gaula.   Uni-
      versity of Iowa, 1963.

466   Flam, Bernard P.   A concordance to the works of Auzias
      March.   University of Wisconsin, 1962.

467   Flaume, Anatol.   Make-up of a textbook for an intensive
      Russian course.   University of Pennsylvania, 1960.

468   Fleischmann, Charlotte C.   The strong verb in Martin
      Opitz.   University of Pennsylvania, 1921.

469   Flint, Paul H.   Lexical stability in English with par-
      ticular reference to the loss of Old English weak verbs.
      Harvard University, 1948.

470   Flom, George T.   Scandinavian influence on Southern
      Lowland Scotch: A contribution to the study of the
      linguistic relations of English and Scandinavian.
      Columbia University, 1900.

471   Flores, Francisco G.   A contrastive analysis of selected
      clause types of Cebuano and English.   University of
      Michigan, 1963

472   Flum, Philip N., Jr.   An etymological dictionary of the
      Friulian dialect of Raeto-Romance.   University of North
      Carolina, 1953.

473   Fodale, Peter.   The Sicilian dialects as a diasystem:
      A study in structural dialectology.   University of
      Michigan, 1964.

474   Foley, Emily H.   The language of the Northumbrian gloss
      to the Gospel of Saint Matthew.   Yale University, 1902.

475   Folk, Lucile P.   A word atlas of North Louisiana.   Loui-
      siana State University, 1961.

476   Folsom, Marvin H.   The syntax of substantive and non-
      finite satellites to the finite verb in German.   Cornell
      University, 1961.

477   Foote, Stefanie von S.   Syntactic structures of modern
      German.   Radcliffe College, 1962.

478   Forchheimer, Paul.   The category of person in language.
      Columbia University, 1951.

479   Ford, Gordon B., Jr.   A phonological, morphological and
      syntactical investigation of the Old Lithuanian Cate-
      chism of Baltramiejus Vilentas (1579).   Harvard Univer-
      sity, 1964.

480   Ford, Harry E.   Modern Provençal phonology and morphology
      studied in the language of Frederic Mistral.   Columbia
      University, 1921.

481   Forsyth, John.   Phonemic structures of Medieval Spanish
      as reflected in the Libro de buen amor.   University of
      New Mexico, 1961.

482   Foster, Harry K.   The semantic variation of certain high
      frequency words in the written compositions of eighth-
      grade pupils.   University of Iowa, 1940.

483   Foster, Richard H.   The Spanish in the Cebuano vocabu-
      lary of the Bible as a partial revelation of Spanish
      cultural, political, and economic influence in the
      Philippine Islands.   University of California at
      Berkeley, 1948.

484   Foster, Walter E.   Studies in archaism in Aulus Gellius.
      Columbia University, 1912.

485   Fotitch, Tatiana Z.   The narrative tenses in Chrétien
      de Troyes: A study in syntax and stylistics.   Catholic
      University of America, 1950.

486   Foulkrod, Emily.   Compounds of the word 'horse': A study
      in semantics.   University of Pennsylvania, 1919.

487   Fowkes, Robert A.   Gothic etymological studies.   Colum-
      bia University, 1949.

488   Fowler, Alexander M.   Expressions for immortality in the
      early Indo-European languages, with special references
      to Homer, the Rig-Veda, and the poetic Edda.   Harvard
      University, 1940.

489   Frachtenberg, Leo J.   Grammar of the Coos language of
      Oregon.   Columbia University, 1910.

490   Fraenkel, Gerd. A generative grammar of Azerbaijani.
      Indiana University, 1962.

491   Francis, Henry E. The adjectives of Donne and Wordsworth:
      The key to a poetic quality. University of Southern
      California, 1964.

492   Frank, Francine H. Taxemic redundancy in Spanish. Uni-
      versity of Illinois, 1955.

493   Frank, Marcella. A manual for teaching sentence struc-
      ture through practice in the college composition/communi-
      cation course. Columbia University, 1963.

494   Frank, Yakira H. The speech of New York City. Univer-
      sity of Michigan, 1949.

495   Frankart, J.D. Grammaticalness: Its psychological di-
      mension and relation to habit. Ohio State University,
      1963.

496   Frankle, Eleanor. Word formation in the Turkic lan-
      guages. Columbia University, 1948.

497   Frary, Louise G. Studies in the syntax of the Old Eng-
      lish passive with special reference to the use of wesan
      and weorðan. University of Minnesota, 1926.

498   Frayha, Anis K. Quadriliterals from the dialect of Ras
      al-Matn. University of Chicago, 1936.

499   Freed, Lewis M. The sources of Johnson's Dictionary.
      Cornell University, 1939.

500   Freedman, David N. The evolution of early Hebrew ortho-
      graphy: The epigraphic evidence. Johns Hopkins Univer-
      sity, 1948.

501   Frei, Ernest J. Tagalog as the Philippine national lan-
      guage. Hartford Seminary Foundation, 1947.

502   French, Howard P. The secondary verb in Middle High
      German and New High German. Indiana University, 1952.

503   Frey, Herschel J. A comparative phonology of medieval
      and modern Spanish: El libro de buen amor. University
      of North Carolina at Chapel Hill, 1963.

504   Frey, John W.   The German dialect of Eastern York County,
      Pennsylvania.   University of Illinois, 1942.

505   Friedman, Henrietta K.   The personal pronoun in the
      Geste des Loherains.   New York University, 1960.

506   Friend, Joseph H.   The development of American lexico-
      graphy from its beginning through the Webster-Worcester
      dictionary war.   Indiana University, 1962.

507   Frierson, David E.   A historical study of the language
      of Venice XIII, Franco-Italian manuscript of the four-
      teenth century.   University of North Carolina, 1937.

508   Fries, Charles C.   The periphrastic future with shall
      and will in modern English.   University of Michigan,
      1922.

509   Fries, Peter H.   The uses of the infinitive in the ob-
      ject of the verb in English.   University of Pennsylvania,
      1964.

510   Frink, Orrin.   Verbal government in the Old Russian Pri-
      mary Chronicle.   Harvard University, 1961.

511   Frith, James R.   Some statistical aspects of French
      suffixation.   Cornell University, 1950.

512   Frogen, George H.   The change from the Attic to the
      Ionic alphabet in Athenian decrees (circa 570 to 317
      B.C.).   University of Minnesota, 1955.

513   Fry, Morton A.H.   The suffixes man, van, min, and vin
      in Sanskrit.   Princeton University, 1935.

514   Funk, Henry E.   The French Creole dialect of Martinique:
      Its historical background, vocabulary, syntax, proverbs,
      and literature with a glossary.   University of Virginia,
      1953.

515   Funk, Robert W.   The syntax of the Greek article: Its
      importance for critical Pauline problems.   Vanderbilt
      University, 1954.

516   Gaenssel, Carl.   The Hebrew particle אשר.   University of
      Chicago, 1914.

517   Gage, William W.   Grammatical structures in American
      intonation.   Cornell University, 1958.

518 Gair, James W. Clause structures in spoken colloquial
     Sinhalese. Cornell University, 1963.

519 Gallary, Leo N. The Latinity of the Dacian inscriptions.
     Harvard University, 1940.

520 Galline, Francis E. The influence of the Baltic lan-
     guages on the German languages in East Prussia. Harvard
     University, 1940.

521 Galvan, Robert A. El dialecto español de San Antonio,
     Texas. Tulane University, 1955.

522 Gamal-Eldin, Saad M. A syntactic study of Colloquial
     Egyptian Arabic. University of Texas, 1961.

523 Ganss, George E. Parataxis by means of kai in the
     Gospel of St. Luke. St. Louis University, 1934.

524 Garbutt, Cameron W. A study of the dialectal character-
     istics of the older generation living in the three
     southernmost counties of Illinois: Alexander, Pulaski,
     and Massac. Louisiana State University, 1952.

525 Garcia, Erica C. History of the English tense system.
     Columbia University, 1964.

526 Garcia-Girón, Edmundo. The adjective: A contribution
     to the study of modernist poetic diction. University
     of California at Berkeley, 1952.

527 Gardner, Elizabeth F. The inflections of modern liter-
     ary Japanese. Yale University, 1948.

528 Gardner, Rosalyn H. Studies in fourteenth-century
     French syntax. University of North Carolina, 1950.

529 Garey, Howard B. The historical development of tenses
     from Late Latin to Old French. Yale University, 1953.

530 Garfield, Eugene E. An algorithm for translating chemi-
     cal names to molecular formulas. University of Pennsyl-
     vania, 1961.

531 Garner, John E. A descriptive study of the phonology of
     Acadian French. University of Texas, 1952.

532 Garvey, Sister M. Calixta. A syntactical study of the
     declinable words in the Roman de la Rose. Catholic Uni-
     versity of America, 1936.

533 Garvin, Paul L. Kutenai grammar. Indiana University, 1947.

534 Gattiker, Godfrey L. The syntactic basis of the poetic formula in **Beowulf**. University of Wisconsin, 1962.

535 Gavigan, John J. The syntax of the Gesta Francorum. University of Pennsylvania, 1943.

536 Gebauer, George J. Prolegomena to the Ars Grammatica Bonifatii. University of Chicago, 1941.

537 Gebert, Otto C. Les termes techniques militaires dans les traductions françaises de Végèce. Stanford University, 1920.

538 Gedney, William J. Indic loanwords in spoken Thai. University of Washington, 1947.

539 Geer, Russel M. Quatenus vita Vergitiana Aelio Donato attributa re vera Suetonio Tranquillo debeatur quaeritur. Harvard University, 1926.

540 Geisness, Thomas. Comparative study of words denoting joy and grief in the Gothic, Old English, and Old Saxon, with reference to corresponding words and expressions in Greek and Latin. University of Minnesota, 1902.

541 Gerdes, Sister Florence M. The language of the Roman Missal. St. Louis University, 1958.

542 Gerhard, George B. A dictionary of Middle English musical terms. Indiana University, 1961.

543 Gerhard, Robert H. Japanese pronunciation. University of Ohio, 1946.

544 Gerow, Edwin M. A glossary of Indian figures of speech. University of Chicago, 1963.

545 Gerrard, Allen G. A study of the usage of the Spanish locative adverbs, aquí and acá. University of Michigan, 1963.

546 Ghaly, Muhammad M. Substantive morphology of Colloquial Egyptian Arabic. University of Michigan, 1960.

547 Ghigo, Francis. The vocabulary of Mellin de Saint-Gelays. University of North Carolina, 1943.

548   Giacumakis, George, Jr.   The Akkadian of Alalakh.   Bran-
       deis University, 1963.

549   Gibbon, William B.   Popular star names among the Slavic
       speaking peoples.   University of Pennsylvania, 1960.

550   Gienapp, Norman.   Paired expressions in Homer.   Univer-
       sity of Illinois, 1957.

551   Giesecke, Gustav E.   Loan-translation in German as the
       linguistic conquest of foreign semantic fields.   Uni-
       versity of Pittsburgh, 1939.

552   Gifford, Clarence W.   The vocabulary of American history.
       University of Wisconsin, 1928.

553   Gilbert, Glenn G.   The German dialect spoken in Kendall
       and Gillespie Counties, Texas.   Harvard University,
       1963.

554   Gill, Harjeet S.   A descriptive grammar of Panjabi.
       Hartford Seminary Foundation, 1962.

555   Gillis, Carroll O.   The Greek participle in the doctrinal
       Epistles of Paul.   Southwestern Baptist Theological
       Seminary, 1937.

556   Gillis, Rev. John H.   The coordinating particles in
       Saints Hilary, Jerome, Ambrose, and Augustine.   Catholic
       University of America, 1939.

557   Gilman, Wayne C., Jr.   A lexical analysis of the prose
       writings of Jean Giono.   Tulane University, 1957.

558   Gimborn, Bro. D. Thomas.   The syntax of the simple cases
       in St. Hilary of Poitiers.   Catholic University of
       America, 1938.

559   Giuffrida, Robert T.   The adjective in the works of
       Notker.   George Washington University, 1958.

560   Glazer, Sidney S.   Abu Hayyan's commentary to the _Alfiyya_
       of Ibn Malik: Studies in the grammatical literature of
       the Arabs.   Yale University, 1937.

561   Glenn, Jessie M.   The neuter plural in iambic and trochaic
       verse.   University of Pennsylvania, 1939.

562   Glenn, Robert B. Linguistic class-indicators in the
      speech of Dickens' characters. University of Michigan,
      1961.

563   Gminder, Albert. A study in fourteenth-century Spanish
      syntax. University of North Carolina, 1959.

564   Goddard, Burton L. The origin of the Hebrew infinitive
      absolute in the light of infinitive uses in related
      languages and its use in the Old Testament. Harvard
      University, 1950.

565   Godfrey, Robert G. The development of theoretical
      grammar in the Middle Ages, with special attention to
      the work of Thomas of Erfurt. University of Kentucky,
      1956.

566   Goetchius, Eugene V. Palatalization in Germanic. Uni-
      versity of Virginia, 1949.

567   Goff, Marie E. The language of the eighth-century docu-
      ments of central Italy. Columbia University, 1958.

568   Gokey, Rev. Francis X. The terminology for the devil
      and evil spirits in the Apostolic Fathers. Catholic
      University of America, 1961.

569   Golden, Ruth W.I. Effectiveness of instructional tapes
      for changing regional speech patterns. Wayne State
      University, 1963.

570   Golson, Eva O. The spelling system of the Glasgow MS
      of The Canterbury Tales. University of Chicago, 1942.

571   Goodison, Ronald A.C. The phonology of Czech. Cornell
      University, 1952.

572   Goodloe, Jane F. Nomina agentis auf -el im Neuhoch-
      deutschen. Johns Hopkins University, 1927.

573   Goodman, Allan C. Imitation of intonation patterns.
      University of Michigan, 1952.

574   Goodman, John S. The syntax of the verb 'to be' in
      Malory's prose. University of Michigan, 1962.

575   Goodman, Morris F. A comparative study of Creole French.
      Columbia University, 1961.

576   Goodstein, Moses. The Judeo-Arabic book of philological comparisons between Hebrew, Aramaic and Arabic, known as the Risala of Judah Ibn Quraish. Yeshiva University, 1960.

577   Goodwin, Reason A. Contrasts of case and of adjective form in Russian predicate noun and adjective constructions. University of Chicago, 1952.

578   Gordon, Alan M. Verb-creation in the works of José Martí: Method and function. Harvard University, 1956.

579   Gordon, Barbara Y. An application of the findings of structural linguistics to the teaching of English in the lower elementary grades: An exploratory study. Columbia University, 1962.

580   Gordon, Clavin G. The subjunctive mood in representative Spanish authors from the twelfth to the eighteenth century. University of Nebraska, 1964.

581   Gosser, Leo. Some studies in the vocabulary of Old English. University of Chicago, 1926.

582   Gottlieb, Eugene. A systematic tabulation of Indo-European animal names, with special reference to their etymology and semasiology. New York University, 1930.

583   Gould, Chester N. The syntax of at and ana in Gothic, Old Saxon, and Old High German. University of Chicago, 1907.

584   Grace, George W. The position of the Polynesian languages within the Austronesian (Malayo-Polynesian) language family. Columbia University, 1958.

585   Graham, Robert S. Bilingualism and the creative writer of French Canada. University of Colorado, 1955.

586   Grant, Clyde M. A vocabulary study of Skeat's edition of the A-text of Piers Plowman. University of Oklahoma, 1956.

587   Graves, Eugene V. The Old Cornish vocabulary. Columbia University, 1962.

588   Grayson, John D. The remains of inflection in Afrikaans. New York University, 1962.

589 Green, Alexander. The dative of agency: A chapter of
     Indo-European case-syntax. Columbia University, 1913.

590 Green, Carleton. The place-names in the Historia
     Ecclesiastica of Bede. Harvard University, 1936.

591 Green, Corinne W. Word studies in the Consolatio at-
     tributed to Cicero together with an index verborum.
     University of North Carolina, 1948.

592 Green, Eugene. Yiddish and English in Detroit: A sur-
     vey and analysis of reciprocal influences in bilinguals'
     pronunciation, grammar, and vocabulary. University of
     Michigan, 1962.

593 Green, James R. A comparison of the oral and written
     language: A quantitative analysis of the structure and
     vocabulary of the oral and written language of a group
     of college students. New York University, 1958.

594 Greene, Marion A. Studies in fifteenth-century French
     syntax. University of North Carolina, 1950.

595 Greenfield, Jonas C. The lexical status of Mishnaic
     Hebrew. Yale University, 1956.

596 Greis, Naguib A.F. The pedagogical implications of a
     contrastive analysis of cultivated Cairene Arabic and
     the English language. University of Minnesota, 1963.

597 Gries, Konrad. Constancy in Livy's Latinity. Columbia
     University, 1949.

598 Griffin, George R. Forms and uses of address in Plautus.
     Marquette University, 1943.

599 Griggs, Silas, Jr. The potential-substitution distribu-
     tion: A tool for stylistic research. University of
     Texas, 1963.

600 Grimes, Joseph E. Huichol syntax. Cornell University,
     1960.

601 Grubb, Patti M. A psychophysical study of vowel for-
     mants. University of Illinois, 1956.

602 Gruen, Ferdinand B. English grammar in American high
     schools since 1900. Catholic University of America, 1934.

603 Gudschinsky, Sarah C. Proto-Popotecan: A comparative
     study of Popolocan and Mixtecan. University of Pennsyl-
     vania, 1958.

604 Guentherodt, Ingrid. A phonological analysis of French
     loanwords in the Palatinate dialect. University of
     Texas, 1964.

605 Guilbeau, John J. The French spoken in Lafourche Parish,
     Louisiana. University of North Carolina, 1952.

606 Guiliano, Vincent E. An experimental study of automatic
     language translation. Harvard University, 1959.

607 Guinn, Lawrence E. English runes and runic writing: The
     development of the runes and their employment. Univer-
     sity of Pennsylvania, 1959.

608 Gummere, John F. The neuter plural in Vergil. Univer-
     sity of Pennsylvania, 1933.

609 Gumperz, John J. The Swabian dialect of Washtenaw
     County, Michigan. University of Michigan, 1954.

610 Gunter, Richard L. Elliptical forms in the English
     transitive sentence. Indiana University, 1962.

611 Gurren, Louise. A comparison on a phonetic basis of the
     two chief languages of the Americas, English and Spanish.
     New York University, 1955.

612 Guss, Evelyn G. A study of the vocabulary of Aristophanes'
     Plutus. University of Pittsburgh, 1962.

613 Gustafson, Walter W. The Swedish language in the United
     States. New York University, 1929.

614 Haase, Gladys D. Spenser's orthography: An examination
     of a poet's use of the variant pronunciations of Eliz-
     abethan English. Columbia University, 1952.

615 Haden, Ernest F. The physiology of French consonant
     changes: A study in experimental phonetics. University
     of Chicago, 1937.

616 Hadlich, Roger L. The phonological history of Vegliote.
     University of Michigan, 1961.

617 Hagen, Sivert N. The Norse loan-words in the York
     mystery plays. Johns Hopkins University, 1900.

618   Haggard, Elias M. Syllable stress in French words as
      used by Chaucer and Spenser. George Peabody College
      for Teachers, 1944.

619   Hagopian, John V. The morphology of John Donne includ-
      ing a pun index, rhyme index, and studies in the rela-
      tions between linguistics and literature. Western Re-
      serve University, 1956.

620   Hagstrom, Elaine K.R. Samoyed phonemic systems. Indi-
      ana University, 1960.

621   Hakeda, Yoshito. Characteristics of the language of the
      epics of Aśvaghoṣa, especially as compared with that of
      the epics of Kālidāsa. Yale University, 1960.

622   Hale, Kenneth L. A Papago grammar. Indiana Univer-
      sity, 1959.

623   Haley, Joseph B. Some modal uses in the papyri. Uni-
      versity of Wisconsin, 1921.

624   Hall, Joseph S. The phonetics of Great Smoky Mountain
      speech. Columbia University, 1942.

625   Halle, Morris. The Russian consonants: A phonemic and
      acoustical investigation. Harvard University, 1955.

626   Hallo, William W. Early Mesopotamian royal titles: A
      philologic and historical analysis. University of
      Chicago, 1956.

627   Hallock, Richard T. The Chicago syllabary and the Louvre
      syllabary A07661. University of Chicago, 1934.

628   Halstead, William P. A study of the factor of vari-
      ability in the perception of speech melody. University
      of Michigan, 1935.

629   Halvorson, Henry G.H. A study of Old English dithematic
      personal names: Deuterothemes. Harvard University, 1937.

630   Hamblen, Albert A. An investigation to determine the
      extent to which the effect of the study of Latin upon
      a knowledge of English derivatives can be increased by
      conscious adaptation of content and method to the attain-
      ment of the objective. University of Pennsylvania, 1925.

631   Hamilton, Alfred. Compounds of the word 'cow': A study
      in semantics. Pennsylvania State University, 1923.

632 Hammond, Mac S. Sound and grammar in Wallace Stevens'
     The Man with the Blue Guitar. Harvard University, 1962.

633 Hamp, Eric P. Vaccarizzo Albanese phonology: The sound-
     system of a Calabro-Albanian dialect. Harvard Univer-
     sity, 1954.

634 Han, Mieko S. Japanese phonology: An analysis based on
     sound spectrograms. University of Texas, 1961.

635 Haney, John B. The strong verb in Moscherosch. New
     York University, 1935.

636 Hankey, Clyde T. A Colorado word geography. University
     of Michigan, 1960.

637 Hanley, Theodore D. An analysis of vocal frequency and
     duration characteristics of selected samples of speech
     from general American, eastern American and southern
     American dialect regions. University of Iowa, 1950.

638 Hanna, Hanna M. The phrase structure of Egyptian Collo-
     quial Arabic. Cornell University, 1962.

639 Hanna, Sami A. Problems of American college students in
     learning Arabic: A diagnostic study of reading errors,
     remedial instruction, and a proposed method of teaching.
     University of Utah, 1964.

640 Hansen, Carl V. The impersonal construction in Old
     Norse. Yale University, 1952.

641 Hansen, Robert E. Theophorous son names among the
     Arameans and their neighbors. Johns Hopkins University,
     1948.

642 Hanzeli, Victor E. Early descriptions by French mission-
     aries of Algonquin and Iroquoian languages: A study of
     seventeenth- and eighteenth-century practice in linguis-
     tics. Indiana University, 1961.

643 Harbold, James G. Recognition of three magnitudes of
     interphonemic transitional influence. Ohio State Uni-
     versity, 1955.

644 Harder, Jayne C. The influence of the teaching of elo-
     cution on modern English pronunciation. University of
     Florida, 1956.

645   Hardigree, Cruz A.C.F.   Effects of selected phonetic
      aspects in the transmission of the Spanish language.
      Ohio State University, 1957.

646   Hardison, Aura D.   The syntax of the verb in Jean Rotrou's
      dramatic works.   University of Southern California, 1936.

647   Hardman, Martha J.   Jaqara: Outline of phonological and
      morphological structure.   Stanford University, 1963.

648   Hardy, William G.   Some semantic theories.   Cornell Uni-
      versity, 1943.

649   Hargis, Donald E.   A study of the vocabulary of the
      radio.   University of Michigan, 1944.

650   Harms, Robert T.   A descriptive grammar of Estonian.
      University of Chicago, 1960.

651   Harrell, Richard S.   The phonology of Colloquial Egyptian
      Arabic.   Harvard University, 1956.

652   Harrington, Ronald V.   The language of The Life of St.
      Symeon by Stefan Provencani.   Harvard University, 1964.

653   Harris, Charles C.   Papiamentu phonology.   Cornell Uni-
      versity, 1952.

654   Harris, David P.   The phonemic patterning of the initial
      and final consonant clusters of English from late Old
      English to the present: A structural approach to their
      historical development.   University of Michigan, 1954.

655   Harris, William.   Indo-European -u- formations: A study
      in verb and noun types.   Harvard University, 1952

656   Harris, Zellig S.   A grammar of the Phoenician language.
      University of Pennsylvania, 1934.

657   Harrison, Gordon W.   A study of the range and frequency
      of constructions involving pronouns and pronominal
      adjectives in manuscript J-1, Biblioteca Nacional, of
      the Gran Conquista de Ultramar.   University of Chicago,
      1941.

658   Harsh, Wayne C.   A historical study of the English sub-
      junctive.   University of California at Berkeley, 1963.

659   Hartmann, Jacob W. The Gongu-Hrólfssaga, a study in Old
       Norse philology. Columbia University, 1912.

660   Hartsook, Elisabeth S. Studies on the language of Wil-
       helm Raabe. University of Illinois, 1940.

661   Hartzell, George W. The verb in Duke Julius of Braun-
       schweig's plays. University of Pennsylvania, 1934.

662   Hascall, Edward O., Jr. Predicting success in high
       school foreign language study. University of Michigan,
       1959.

663   Haskell, Ann S. The representation of Gullah-influenced
       dialect in twentieth-century South Carolina prose: 1920-
       30. University of Pennsylvania, 1964.

664   Hasselmo, Nils. American Swedish: A study in bilingual-
       ism. Harvard University, 1961.

665   Hauber, Sister Rose M. The Late Latin vocabulary of the
       Moralia of St. Gregory the Great: A morphological and
       semasiological study. Catholic University of America,
       1939.

666   Haupt, Alden M. Problems in the investigation of Dutch
       influence on the Russian vocabulary. Columbia Univer-
       sity, 1953.

667   Hause, Helen E. Terms for musical instruments in the
       Sudanic languages: A lexicographical inquiry. Univer-
       sity of Pennsylvania, 1947.

668   Hawkins, Jane D. The speech of the Hudson River Valley.
       Brown University, 1941.

669   Hayes, Curtis W. A linguistic analysis of the prose
       style of Edward Gibbon. University of Texas, 1964.

670   Hayes, Kiffin R. A study of the clausulae in Cicero's
       philosophical works. University of North Carolina, 1953.

671   Head, Brian F. A comparison of the segmental phonology
       of Lisbon and Rio de Janeiro. University of Texas, 1964.

672   Heath, James M. Studies in Greek personal and demonstra-
       tive pronouns based on the text of Thucydides (Volumes I
       and II). Princeton University, 1964.

673   Heffner, Edward H.   The sequence of tenses in Plautus.
      University of Pennsylvania, 1916.

674   Heffner, Roe-Merrill S.   The language of the Frankfurt
      Passion Play and its relation to the Frankfurt dialect
      and to standard German.   Harvard University, 1925.

675   Heflin, Woodford A.   Characteristic features of New
      Mexico English between 1805 and 1890.   University of
      Chicago, 1942.

676   Heidel, Alexander.   The quadriliteral verb in Akkadian.
      University of Chicago, 1937.

677   Hejtmanek, Lillian.   The syntax of the exclamation in
      colloquial Mexican.   University of Illinois, 1948.

678   Held, Moshe.   Studies in Ugaritic lexicography and
      poetic style.   Johns Hopkins University, 1957.

679   Held, Warren H., Jr.   The Hittite relative sentence.
      Yale University, 1955.

680   Heller, Louis G.   English linguistic terminology: 995-
      1645.   Columbia University, 1960.

681   Helmy-Hassan, Salah E.   Verb morphology of Egyptian
      Colloquial Arabic (Cairene dialect).   University of
      Michigan, 1960.

682   Hendricks, Ira K.   A historical study of the grammatical
      nomenclature pertaining to the English verb.   Stanford
      University, 1941.

683   Hendriksen, Daniel P.   The effect of extra-phonological
      variables on the hearer's choice of phonemes.   Univer-
      sity of Michigan, 1963.

684   Hendrickson, John R.   Old English prepositional com-
      pounds in relationship to their Latin originals.   Uni-
      versity of Pennsylvania, 1947.

685   Hennes, Rev. William R.   The Latinity of Peter the
      Venerable's De miraculis libri duo.   St. Louis Univer-
      sity, 1937.

686   Henning, William A.   Phoneme discrimination training in
      the teaching of French pronunciation.   Indiana Univer-
      sity, 1964.

687 Henningsen, Caroline H. The East Frisian dialect of
     Point Pleasant, Sacramento County, California. Univer-
     sity of California at Berkeley, 1954.

688 Henry, Collice. The language of the Culex, a poem of
     the Appendix Vergiliana. Stanford University, 1927.

689 Henry, Marten A. Intensity and grammatical meaning,
     studied with special reference to the grammar of German.
     Harvard University, 1938.

690 Hergenhan, Mildred E. The doctrine of correctness in
     English usage in the nineteenth century. University of
     Wisconsin, 1939.

691 Herold, Curtis P. The morphology of King Alfred's trans-
     lation of the Orosius. Indiana University, 1961.

692 Herr, Margaret W. The additional short syllables in
     Ovid. University of Pennsylvania, 1937.

693 Herron, Sister Margaret C. The clausulae of St. Jerome.
     Catholic University of America, 1937.

694 Herzog, Marvin. The Yiddish language in northern Poland:
     Its geography and history. Columbia University, 1964.

695 Hess, Harold H. The syntactic structure of Mezquital
     Otomi. University of Michigan, 1962.

696 Hewitt, Ryland H., Jr. The pronunciation of English in
     the province of Maine, 1636-1730. Cornell University,
     1961.

697 Hibbitt, George W. Diphthongs in American speech: A
     study of the duration of diphthongs in the contextual
     speech of two hundred and ten male undergraduates.
     Columbia University, 1948.

698 Hickerson, Nancy P. An acoustic analysis of Shawnee
     speech. Indiana University, 1957.

699 Highfill, Robert D. The vocabulary of Samuel Sewall
     from 1673 to 1699. University of Chicago, 1927.

700 Hildum, Donald C. Some linguistic measurements and per-
     sonality. Harvard University, 1960.

701   Hill, John. A contribution to Old Spanish lexicography.
      University of Wisconsin, 1913.

702   Hill, Laurita A. A glossary of the marginal homilies of
      MS 41, Corpus Christi College, Cambridge. University of
      Texas, 1947.

703   Hillhouse, Mildred L. Studies in the relationship of
      thought and syntax in colloquial English. University of
      Chicago, 1924.

704   Hills, Sidney O. A semantic and conceptual study of the
      root kpr in the Hebrew Old Testament, with special refer-
      ence to the Accadian Kuppuru. Johns Hopkins University,
      1954.

705   Hilmer, Hermann. Schallnachahmung, Wortschöpfung und
      Bedeutungswandel auf Grundlage der Wahrnehmungen von
      Schlag, Fall, Bruch und derartigen Vorgängen, dargestellt
      an einigen Lautwurzeln der deutschen und der englischen
      Sprache. Stanford University, 1912.

706   Hirsch, Ruth. A study of some aspects of a Judeo-Spanish
      dialect as spoken by a New York Sephardic family. Uni-
      versity of Michigan, 1951.

707   Hoà, Nguyễn D. Verbal and non-verbal patterns of respect-
      behavior in Vietnamese society: Some metalinguistic data.
      New York University, 1956.

708   Hodge, Carleton T. Phonology and morphology of the noun
      and verb in Hausa. University of Pennsylvania, 1943.

709   Hodnett, John J. A study of the Latinity of the Sermones
      and the Carmina of Peter the Venerable, ninth abbot of
      Cluny. St. Louis University, 1938.

710   Hoey, George W.P. The use of the optative mood in the
      works of St. Gregory of Myssa. Catholic University of
      America, 1930.

711   Hoijer, Harry. Tonkawa, an Indian language of Texas.
      University of Chicago, 1931.

712   Holmes, Henry B. An etymological vocabulary of Calila y
      Dimna. University of Wisconsin, 1936.

713   Holt, Anatol W.   A mathematical and applied investiga-
      tion of tree structures for computer linguistic anal-
      ysis.   University of Pennsylvania, 1963.

714   Holzapfel, Tamara O.   The Antioquian dialect of Tomás
      Carrasquilla.   State University of Iowa, 1964.

715   Honsa, Vladimir.   La Gran Conquista de Ultramar, Book
      IV, Chapters 126-193: Critical edition, grammatical
      analysis, and glossary.   University of Michigan, 1957.

716   Hoogstraet, Rev. Arthur F.   The vocabulary of Pope
      Calixtus II in his Epistolae et privilegia.   St. Louis
      University, 1937.

717   Hopkins, Grace S.   Indo-European *deiwos and related
      words.   Yale University, 1931.

718   Hopkins, Melville.   Frontier speech.   Pennsylvania State
      University, 1951.

719   Hopper, Henry P.   A study of the function of the verbal
      prefix ge- in the Lindisfarne Gospel of Saint Matthew.
      George Washington University, 1956.

720   Horn, Robert C.   The use of the subjunctive and optative
      moods in the non-literary papyri.   University of Pennsyl-
      vania, 1926.

721   Hostetter, Winifred H.   A linguistic study of the Vulgar
      Greek Life of Aesop.   University of Illinois, 1955.

722   Howren, Robert R., Jr.   The speech of Louisville, Ken-
      tucky.   Indiana University, 1958.

723   Hoy, Albert L.   An etymological glossary of the East
      Yorkshire dialect, Volumes I and II.   Michigan State
      University, 1956.

724   Hoyt, James.   Korean literature: The rise of the vernac-
      ular, 1443-1592.   University of California at Berkeley,
      1962.

725   Hrdlicka, Clement L.   A study of the Late Latin vocabu-
      lary and of the prepositions and demonstrative pronouns
      in the Confessions of St. Augustine.   Catholic Univer-
      sity of America, 1931.

726   Hubbell, Allan F.   The pronunciation of English in New
      York City: Consonants and vowels. Columbia University,
      1951.

727   Huff, Lloyd D.   Place-names in Chaucer.   Indiana Univer-
      sity, 1950.

728   Hughes, John P.   A phonemic description of the Aran dia-
      lect of modern Irish, with a detailed consideration of
      the problems of palatalization. Columbia University,
      1952.

729   Huguenin, Julian.   Secondary stress in Anglo-Saxon.
      Johns Hopkins University, 1900.

730   Hull, Adrian L.   The linguistic accommodation of a cul-
      tural innovation as illustrated by the game of baseball
      in the Spanish language of Puerto Rico. Columbia Uni-
      versity, 1963.

731   Hull, Alexander, Jr.   The Franco-Canadian dialect of
      Windsor, Ontario: A preliminary study. University of
      Washington, 1955.

732   Hull, Alexander P., Jr.   A semantic and etymological
      study of certain Germanic words for naturally-occurring
      streams of fresh water. University of Virginia, 1955.

733   Humbert, Sister Agnes M.   Verbal repetition in the Ancren
      riwle. Catholic University of America, 1944.

734   Humphreys, Harold L.   A study of dates and causes of
      case reduction in the Old French pronoun. Columbia Uni-
      versity, 1932.

735   Humphries, William J.   An edition and study, linguistic
      and historical, of the French translation of 1372 by
      Jean Corbechon of Book XV (Geography) of Bartholomaeus
      Anglicus' De proprietatibus rerum. University of Cali-
      fornia at Berkeley, 1956.

736   Hungerford, Harlan M.   The verb head construction and
      its modificational patterns in present-day English, with
      special reference to the marked infinitive and single
      word verbs. University of Michigan, 1950.

737   Hungerford, Harold R., Jr.   Comparative constructions in
      the work of Sir Thomas Malory: A synchronic study. Uni-
      versity of California at Berkeley, 1963.

738 Hunsberger, Byron K. Types of error in Latin word knowl-
     edge. University of Pennsylvania, 1932.

739 Hunter, Edwin R. The American colloquial idiom, 1830-
     1860. University of Chicago, 1925.

740 Hursky, Jacob P. The patronymic surnames in Ukrainian.
     University of Pennsylvania, 1957.

741 Hurwitz, Soloman T.H. Root-determinatives in Semitic
     speech: A contribution to Semitic philology. Columbia
     University, 1913.

742 Hutchins, Lucy. The position of the demonstrative adjec-
     tives in Plautus and Terence. University of Chicago,
     1937.

743 Hutson, Arthur E. The British Latin sources and the
     British personal names in the Historia Regum Britanniae
     of Geoffrey of Monmouth. University of California, 1934.

744 Huttar, David K. Conditional sentences in Coptic.
     Brandeis University, 1962.

745 Hymes, Dell H. The language of the Kathlamet Chinook.
     Indiana University, 1955.

746 Iannucci, James E. Lexical number in Spanish nouns with
     reference to English equivalents. University of Pennsyl-
     vania, 1951.

747 Idol, Harriett R. A strobophotographic study of Southern
     intonation. Louisiana State University, 1937.

748 Ihrig, Roscoe M. The semantic development of words for
     'walk, run' in the Germanic languages. University of
     Chicago, 1914.

749 Ilkow, Peter. Die Nominalkomposita der altsächsischen
     Bibeldichtung: Ein semantisch-kulturgeschichtliches
     Glossar. Harvard University, 1956.

750 Ingemann, Frances. An East Cheremis grammar. Indiana
     University, 1956.

751 Ingledue, Grace E. A study of the speech of the three
     generations in one family, and in like generations of
     three different families in Monroe, Louisiana. Louisi-
     ana State University, 1938.

752   Inoue, Kazuko. A study of Japanese syntax. University
      of Michigan, 1964.

753   Insler, Stanley. Verbal paradigms in Patanjali. Yale
      University, 1963.

754   Ishchuk-Pazuniak, Natalia. The vocative case in Ukrain-
      ian. University of Pennsylvania, 1956.

755   Ives, Sumner A. The dialect of the Uncle Remus stories.
 ✓   University of Texas, 1950.

756   Jackson, Elizabeth H. An analysis of Colorado Atlas
      records with regard to settlement history and other
      factors. University of Colorado, 1956.

757   Jacobs, Melville. A sketch of northern Sahaptin gram-
      mar. University of Washington, 1931.

758   Jacobsen, William H., Jr. A grammar of the Washo lan-
      guage. University of California at Berkeley, 1964.

759   Jansen-Beck, Lydia I. Possessive pronouns in Garin le
      Loheren and Gerbert de Mey. New York University, 1960.

760   Jazayery, Mohammad A. English loan-words in Persian:
      A study in language and culture. University of Texas,
      1958.

761   Jeffers, Coleman R. Medievalisms in the writings of the
      Spanish romanticists. University of Iowa, 1954.

762   Jenkins, Frederic M. French endocentric nominals. Uni-
      versity of California at Berkeley, 1963.

763   Jenkins, Henry H., Jr. The diction of Yank: Colloquial
      speech of the American soldier of World War II as found
      in Yank magazine. University of Florida, 1957.

764   Jennings, Augustus C. A linguistic study of the Cartu-
      lario de San Vicente de Oviedo. Columbia University,
      1941.

765   Jensen, Frede. The syntax of the Old French subjunctive.
      University of California at Los Angeles, 1961.

766   Jinushi, Toshiko S. The structure of Japanese: A study
      based on a restatement of phonology and an analysis of
      inflected words. State University of New York at Buffalo,
      1963.

767   Jofen, Jean B.   The dialectological makeup of East Euro-
      pean Yiddish: Phonological and lexicological criteria.
      Columbia University, 1953.

768   Johannes, Wilfred C.   The people of Menander: A study of
      nouns designating family occupation, social and servile
      class.   University of Michigan, 1963.

769   Johnson, Anne C.   The pronoun of direct address in seven-
      teenth-century English.   Columbia University, 1959.

770   Johnson, Emma W.   Studies in East Armenian grammar.   Uni-
      versity of California at Berkeley, 1954.

771   Johnson, Falk S.   Phonetic alphabets and phonetic texts
      as evidence of American pronunciation before 1850.   Uni-
      versity of Chicago, 1956.

772   Johnson, Irving R.   A study of the Amana (Iowa) dialect.
      University of Iowa, 1936.

773   Johnson, M. Margueritte.   The verbid clause in current
      English.   University of Washington, 1960.

774   Jolin, John J.   A lexicographical and stylistic study
      of the De Incarnatione Jesu Christi Domini Nostri and
      the De Miraculis Sanctae Mariae Lauddunensis of Hermannus
      Tornacensis.   St. Louis University, 1938.

775   Jones, Frank P.   The ad urbe condita construction in
      Greek: A study in the classification of the participle.
      University of Wisconsin, 1937.

776   Jones, Lawrence G.   Acoustic patterns of the Russian
      vowels.   Harvard University, 1952.

777   Jones, Morgan E.   A phonological study of English as
      spoken by Puerto Ricans, contrasted with Puerto Rican
      Spanish and American English.   University of Michigan,
      1962.

778   Jones, Robert B., Jr.   The Karen language: Descriptive
      and comparative studies.   University of California at
      Berkeley, 1958.

779   Jones, William.   Some principles of Algonquin word-
      formation.   Columbia University, 1904.

780   Joos, Martin. Statistical studies in Gothic phonology.
      University of Wisconsin, 1940.

781   Jorden, Eleanor H. The syntax of modern colloquial
      Japanese. Yale University, 1950.

782   Joshi, Shivram D. Kaunda Bhatta on the meaning of the
      Sanskrit verb. Harvard University, 1960.

783   Josselson, Harry H. Stress patterns of noun declension
      in standard Russian. University of Michigan, 1952.

784   Joynes, Mary Lu. Structural analysis of Old English
      metrics. University of Texas, 1958.

785   Jungemann, Frederick H. The substratum theory and the
      Hispano-Romance and Gascon dialects: A functional-
      structural analysis of some phonological problems.
      Columbia University, 1952.

786   Juniper, Walter H. A study of verbs of saying in Plautus.
      University of Ohio, 1937.

787   Juntado, Loreto G. Number concord in English and Hili-
      gaynon. University of Michigan, 1961.

788   Kangasmaa, Eiri E.S. Derivation in Cheremis. Indiana
      University, 1955.

789   Karateew, Nicholas. Morphemes of Russian noun derivation
      on the first level of IC relevancy. Cornell University,
      1953.

790   Kassarjian, Mary Catherine Bateson. A study of linguis-
      tic patterning in pre-Islamic Arabic poetry. Harvard
      University, 1963.

791   Kaufman, Terrence S. Tzeltal grammar. University of
      California at Berkeley, 1963.

792   Keaton, Anna L. Americanisms in early American news-
      papers. University of Chicago, 1933.

793   Kehlenbeck, Alfred P. Die plattdeutsche Mundart in Iowa
      County, Iowa. University of Wisconsin, 1934.

794   Keiser, Albert. The influence of Christianity on the
      vocabulary of Old English poetry. University of Illinois,
      1918.

795 Kek, Anna M.D. _Oportere_, _debere_, _convenire_, _decere_, _necesse esse_, _opus esse_, and _usus esse_ in Republican Latin. Cornell University, 1941.

796 Kelkar, Ashok R. The phonology and morphology of Marathi. Cornell University, 1958.

797 Kellenberger, Hunter. The influence of accentuation on French word order. Princeton University, 1931.

798 Kelley, Emma C. Coordinating symbolic logic with grammatical discourse. New York University, 1953.

799 Kelley, Francis M. The origin of the use of _i_ as a sign of length in Middle Scots. Columbia University, 1957.

800 Kellinger, Josef M. Der Einfluss der französischen Revolution auf den deutschen Wortschatz. Syracuse University, 1952.

801 Kellogg, Allen B. The language of the alliterative _Siege of Jerusalem_. University of Chicago, 1943.

802 Kellum, Margaret D. The language of the Northumbrian Gloss to the Gospel of St. Luke. Yale University, 1905.

803 Kelly, Bro. David H. The word in ancient Greek: A phonological study. University of Pennsylvania, 1958.

804 Kemp, Lorena E. A grammar of the Kentish dialect of Old English. University of Chicago, 1954.

805 Kennedy, Arthur G. The pronoun of address in English literature of the thirteenth century. Leland Stanford University, 1914.

806 Kenny, Hamill T. The origin and meaning of the Indian place-names of Maryland. University of Maryland, 1951.

807 Kenyon, John S. The syntax of the infinitive in Chaucer. Harvard University, 1908.

808 Kerby-Miller, Wilma A. Scribal dialects in the C and D manuscripts of _The Canterbury Tales_. University of Chicago, 1938.

809 Kerns, J. Alexander. Ablaut in the preterite and preterite participle of strong verbs in the West Midland dialect of Middle English. New York University, 1935.

810 Kerns, Jean G. The verbal system of the <u>Annals of Inisfallen</u>. New York University, 1950.

811 Key, E. Mary. Comparative phonology of the Tacanan languages. University of Texas, 1963.

812 Key, Harold H. Morphology of Cayuvava. University of Texas, 1963.

813 Keys, George R. The present tense in the Romance languages, with special reference to French and Italian. University of North Carolina, 1948.

814 Keyser, Samuel J. The dialect of Samuel Worcester. Yale University, 1962.

815 Khalafallah, Abdelghany A. A descriptive grammar of Saʕi:di Colloquial Egyptian Arabic. University of Texas, 1961.

816 Khoury, Joseph F. Arabic teaching manual, with an analysis of the major problems American high school students face in learning Arabic. University of Utah, 1962.

817 Khubchandani, Lachman. The acculturation of Indian Sindhi to Hindi: A study of language in contact. University of Pennsylvania, 1963.

818 Kilpatrick, Rachel S.H. The speech of Rhode Island: The stressed vowels and diphthongs. Brown University, 1937.

819 Kimmerle, Marjorie M. Norwegian surnames of the Koshkonong and Springdale congregations in Dane County, Wisconsin. University of Wisconsin, 1938.

820 Kindschi, Lowell. The Latin-Old English glossaries in Plantin-Moretus MS 32 and British Museum MS Additional 32,246. Stanford University, 1955.

821 King, Harold V. The syntax of nouns in Cato's <u>De agricultura</u>. University of Michigan, 1950.

822 King, James C. Two dualisms in the syntax of Notker Teutonicus. George Washington University, 1954.

823 Kinkade, Marvin D. Phonology and morphology of Upper Chehalis. Indiana University, 1963.

824   Kinnavey, Rev. Raymond J.   The vocabulary of St. Hilary
      of Poitiers as contained in Commentarius in Matthaeum
      liber I ad Constantium and De Trinitate.   Catholic Univer-
      sity of America, 1937.

825   Kinnirey, Sister Ann J.   The Late Latin vocabulary of
      The Dialogues of St. Gregory the Great.   Catholic Uni-
      versity, 1936.

826   Kinzel, Paul F.   A description of lexical and grammati-
      cal interference in the speech of a bilingual child.
      University of Washington, 1964.

827   Kirch, Max S.   Einfluss des Niederdeutschen auf die
      hochdeutsche Schriftsprache.   University of Pennsyl-
      vania, 1951.

828   Kirk, Daniel F.   Charles Dodgson, semeiotician.   Florida
      University at Gainesville, 1959.

829   Kirshner, Harold.   The nature vocabulary of Notker Labeo:
      A study in early German scientific terminology.   New York
      University, 1963.

830   Kirwin, William J., Jr.   Inflectional and principal syn-
      tactic classes in Chaucer's Canterbury Tales.   University
      of Chicago, 1964.

831   Kispert, Robert J.   New Venetic and Messapic inscriptions.
      Harvard University, 1958.

832   Kjelds, Niels T.   Suffixal word derivation in New Danish.
      University of Pennsylvania, 1954.

833   Klagstad, Harold L., Jr.   Vowel-zero alternations in con-
      temporary standard Russian.   Harvard University, 1954.

834   Klatte, William F.   Text and morphology of MS 1 of the
      Österreichische Chronik von den 95 Herrschaften.   Uni-
      versity of Chicago, 1957.

835   Klein, Sheldon.   Automatic decoding of written English.
      University of California at Berkeley, 1963.

836   Kleiner, Mathilde.   Zur Entwicklung der Futurumschreibung
      werden mit dem Infinitiv.   University of California, 1923.

837   Kleinjans, Everett.   A descriptive-comparative study pre-
      dicting interference for the Japanese in learning English

noun-head modification patterns. University of Michigan, 1958.

838   Klimas, Antanas. Primitive Germanic *kuningaz and its spread. University of Pennsylvania, 1956.

839   Knowlton, Edgar C., Jr. Words of Chinese, Japanese, and Korean origin in the Romance languages. Stanford University, 1959.

840   Koban, Charles. Substantive compounds in Beowulf. University of Illinois, 1963.

841   Kobayashi, Eichi. A study of verb forms of the South English Legendary in British Museum MS Harley 2277. University of Michigan, 1962.

842   Kodjak, Andrej. The language of Alexej Remizov. University of Pennsylvania, 1963.

843   Koen, Frank M. Semantic constancy: The stability of word meanings in relation to contextual differences. Vanderbilt University, 1963.

844   Kohmoto, Sutesaburo. Phonemic and subphonemic replacement of English sounds by speakers of Japanese. University of Michigan, 1960.

845   Komai, Akira A. A generative phonology of standard colloquial Japanese. University of Michigan, 1963.

846   Koo, Zung-fung W. Old-English living noun-suffixes exclusive of personal and place-names. Radcliffe College, 1947.

847   Korn, David. Some aspects in the usage of the genitive and accusative cases after negation in contemporary Russian. Georgetown University, 1964.

848   Kosinski, Leonard V. Bilingualism and reading development: A study of the effects of Polish-American bilingualism upon reading achievement in junior high school. University of Wisconsin, 1963.

849   Kosoner, Mordecai. Arabic elements in the Yiddish language of the old Ashkenazic Jewish community in Palestine. Johns Hopkins University, 1947.

850   Koutsoudas, Andreas. Verb morphology of modern Greek: A descriptive analysis. University of Michigan, 1961.

851 Kowacic, Joseph P., Jr. Eine semantische Untersuchung
     des Gotischen und andrer germanischer Dialekte im
     Sinnbezirk des Willens. Bryn Mawr College, 1958.

852 Kozumplik, William A. The phonology of Jacob Ayrer's
     language, based on his rhymes. University of Chicago,
     1942.

853 Kraft, Charles H. A study of Hausa syntax. Hartford
     Seminary Foundation, 1963.

854 Kraft, Walter C. The phonology of Wittenweiler's Ring.
     University of California at Berkeley, 1951.

855 Kramer, Samuel N. The verb in the Kirkuk tablets. Uni-
     versity of Pennsylvania, 1930.

856 Kratz, Henry, Jr. Über den Wortschatz der Erotik im
     Spätmittelhochdeutschen und Frühneuhochdeutschen. Uni-
     versity of Ohio, 1950.

857 Krauss, Michael E. Studies in Irish Gaelic phonology
     and orthography. Harvard University, 1959.

858 Kreidler, Charles W. A study of the influence of Eng-
     lish on the Spanish of Puerto Ricans in Jersey City,
     New Jersey. University of Michigan, 1958.

859 Krishnamurti, Bhadriraju. Telugu verbal bases: A com-
     parative study. University of Pennsylvania, 1957.

860 Kruatrachue, Foongfuang. Thai and English: A compara-
     tive study of phonology for pedagogical applications.
     Indiana University, 1960.

861 Krueger, John R. The structure of discourse and poetry
     in the Mongolian chronicle of Sagang Sechen (1662).
     University of Washington, 1960.

862 Kuehner, Paul. Theories on the origin and formation of
     language in the eighteenth century in France. Univer-
     sity of Pennsylvania, 1941.

863 Kufner, Herbert L. The dialect of the Freutsmoos area
     (Bavaria). Cornell University, 1956.

864 Kuhn, Sherman M. The grammar of the Mercian dialect.
     University of Chicago, 1935.

865   Kuipers, Aert H. A contribution to the analysis of the
       Qabardian language. Columbia University, 1951.

866   Kuno, Susumu. Automatic syntactic analysis of English.
       Harvard University, 1964.

867   Kupsh, Linzey, Jr. The origin of grammatical gender in
       Indo-European. University of Wisconsin, 1962.

868   Kurath, Hans. The semantic sources of the words for the
       emotions in Sanskrit, Greek, Latin and the Germanic lan-
       guages. University of Chicago, 1920.

869   Kyes, Robert L. Old Low Franconian phonology. Univer-
       sity of Michigan, 1964.

870   Kyger, Minor E., Jr. Indo-European words and locutions
       for 'danger' (with emphasis on Germanic and Romance lan-
       guages). Catholic University of America, 1956.

871   Labov, William. The social stratification of English in
       New York City. Columbia University, 1964.

872   Lackowski, Peter G. The formulation of grammatical rules
       in language acquisition. University of Washington, 1964.

873   Laguaite, Jeannette K. Rules for pronunciation of Eng-
       lish orthographic symbols, with practice material.
       Louisiana State University, 1953.

874   Laine, Frank A. The Angevin formulae: A translation
       with linguistic commentary. Vanderbilt University, 1950.

875   Lamb, Sidney M. Mono grammar. University of California
       at Berkeley, 1958.

876   Lamb, William W. The syntax of the Heptameron. New York
       University, 1911.

877   Lambdin, Thomas O. Egyptian loanwords and transcriptions
       in the ancient Semitic languages. Johns Hopkins Univer-
       sity, 1952.

878   Lambert, Roy E. French vocabulary influences in some
       thirteenth-century English works. University of Illinois,
       1957.

879   Lamberts, Jacob J. The dialect of Cursor Mundi (Cotton
       MS Vespasian A III). University of Michigan, 1954.

880   Landar, Herbert J.   Navaho syntax.   Yale University, 1960.

881   Landmark, Nora.   A study of the simple and expanded forms
      of the verb in the present tense.   Michigan State Univer-
      sity, 1954.

882   Landon, George M.   The contribution of grammar to the
      poetic style of Wilfred Owen.   Indiana University, 1964.

883   Landros, Edna.   The Latinity of Isidore of Seville: A
      linguistic study of his Historia Gothorum Vandalorum et
      Suevorum in Hispania.   University of Oregon, 1935.

884   Lane, George S.   Words for clothing in the principal Indo-
      European languages.   University of Chicago, 1930.

885   Langebartel, William W.   The strong verb in the Alammanic
      writings of Rudolf von Tavel.   University of Pennsylvania,
      1949.

886   Langendoen, Donald T.   Modern British linguistics: A study
      of its theoretical and substantive contributions.   Massa-
      chusetts Institute of Technology, 1964.

887   Langworthy, Charles A.   A determination of authorship of
      Henry the Eighth and Two Noble Kinsmen by a comparative
      study of verse-sentence patterns.   University of Michigan,
      1921.

888   Lansberg, William R.   A survey and classification of words
      of uncertain origin in the French language.   University of
      North Carolina, 1945.

889   Lapiken, Peter P.   The language of N.M. Karamzin: A lexico-
      logical study.   University of California at Berkeley, 1953.

890   Lapp, Donald H.   Archaisms in four novels of chivalry.
      State University of Iowa, 1964.

891   Larew, Leonor A.   A study of Spanish articulation in the
      elementary school: A pilot study.   University of Missouri,
      1960.

892   Larry, Etta C.   A study of the sounds of the English lan-
      guage as spoken by five racial groups in the Hawaiian
      Islands.   Columbia University, 1943.

893   Larudee, Faze.   Language teaching in historical perspec-
      tive.   University of Michigan, 1964.

894   Lasley, Marion M. Nominal suffixes in Old Spanish. Co-
      lumbia University, 1953.

895   LaSor, William S. Semitic phonemes with special reference
      to Ugaritic and in the light of the Egyptian evidence.
      Dropsie College, 1949.

896   Lastra, Clementina Y. Cochabamba Quechua syntax. Cornell
      University, 1963.

897   Law, Howard W. Obligatory constructions of Isthmus Nahuat
      grammar. University of Texas, 1962.

898   Lawler, Lillian B. The potential remediability of errors
      in English spelling through the study of high-school
      Latin. University of Iowa, 1925.

899   Lawrence, Vivian S. Dialect mixture in three New England
      pronunciation patterns: Vowels and consonants. Columbia
      University, 1960.

900   Lawson, Dorothy D. The strong verb in Gower's Confessio
      Amantis. New York University, 1953.

901   Lawson, Richard H. A comparative study of the Latin and
      Old High German verb forms in Tatian. University of
      California at Los Angeles, 1957.

902   Lawton, David L. Suprasegmental phenomena in Jamaican
      Creole. Michigan State University, 1963.

903   Leahy, Thomas W. A study of the language in the Essene
      Manual of Discipline. Johns Hopkins University, 1958.

904   Learned, Erma R. Old Portuguese vocalic finals (phonology
      and orthography of accented -ou, -eu, -iu, and -ao, -eo,
      -io). University of Pennsylvania, 1948.

905   Learned, Henry D. The syntax of Brant's Narrenschiff.
      University of Pennsylvania, 1917.

906   Leavitt, Walter D. The position of the object pronouns
      in Old Spanish. Yale University, 1954.

907   Lebow, Daniel B. An historical study of syntax: The evo-
      lution of English from inflectional to prepositional con-
      structions. New York University, 1954.

908   Lee, Donald W. Functional change in early English. Col-
      umbia University, 1947.

909   Lee, Jean L. An etymological dictionary of the Obwaldisch
      dialect of Rhaeto-Romance. University of North Carolina,
      1950.

910   Leed, Richard L. A historical phonology of Czech. Cor-
      nell University, 1958.

911   Lees, Robert B. The grammar of English nominalizations.
      Massachusetts Institute of Technology, 1959.

912   Lefcourt, Ann B. An examination of five elementary Eng-
      lish language textbook series, grades two through eight,
      employing a linguistic scorecard devised for that pur-
      pose. Ball State Teachers College, 1963.

913   Legner, Wolfram K. The strong verb in Sebastian Brant's
      Narrenschiff. University of Pennsylvania, 1936.

914   Lehiste, Ilse. An acoustic-phonetic study of internal
      open juncture. University of Michigan, 1959.

915   Lehmann, Winfred P. The Germanic dental preterite and
      the dh- determinative. University of Wisconsin, 1941.

916   Lehn, Walter I. Rosental Low German: Synchronic and
      diachronic phonology. Cornell University, 1957.

917   Leichty, Verdun E. A critical analysis of present-day
      standardized tests with especial references to the usage
      of the personal pronouns, the absolutes, and the self
      form pronouns, and a comparison of that usage with the
      usage found in purposeful language of the period 1370-
      1910. University of Michigan, 1944.

918   Leiper, Macon A. A diagnostic study of the errors made
      by college freshmen in their written compositions.
      George Peabody College for Teachers, 1926.

919   Lejnieks, Valdis. Mood, tense, and aspect in Homeric
      Greek. Princeton University, 1962.

920   Lelis, Joseph. The place of Latgalian among the Baltic
      dialects. Harvard University, 1961.

921   Lencek, Rado L. The conjugational pattern of contem-
      porary standard Slovene. Harvard University, 1962.

922   Leonard, Clifford S., Jr. A reconstruction of Proto-
      Rhaeto-Romance and its implications for the history of
      French. Cornell University, 1960.

923   Leonard, Sterling A. The doctrine of correctness in Eng-
      lish usage, 1700-1800. University of Wisconsin, 1930.

924   Lester, Mark P. The phonological implications of graphic
      variations in Aelfric's Catholic Homilies. University of
      California at Berkeley, 1964.

925   Leuschel, Donald A. Spanish verb morphology. Indiana
      University, 1960.

926   Levin, Ephraim M. The derivational suffixes of the Rus-
      sian adjective: A synchronic study. Harvard Univ., 1957.

927   Levin, Norman B. The Assiniboine language. University
      of Pennsylvania, 1961.

928   Levin, Samuel R. Negative contractions with Old English
      verbs. University of Pennsylvania, 1956.

929   Levine, Isadore. The language of the Glossary Sangal-
      lensis 912 and its relationship to the language of other
      Latin glossaries. University of Pennsylvania, 1925.

930   Levitt, Jesse. The Grammaire des Grammaires of Girault-
      Duvivier. Columbia University, 1963.

931   Levy, Lawrence J. The Freshman English program of The
      Defiance College: A communications course at a college
      in transition. Columbia University, 1962.

932   Lewis, Charles A. Communication patterns of recent immi-
      grants: A study of three nationality groups in metro-
      politan Detroit. University of Illinois, 1955.

933   Liedke, Otto K. Aktivismus and Passivimus in der erzäh-
      lenden Prosa der modernen deutschen Literatur. Cornell
      University, 1938.

934   Lin, Timonthy T. Egyptian and its Hebraic affinities.
      Dropsie College, 1954.

935   Lincoff, Beatrice. A study in inflectional morphological
      development: Old and Middle Yiddish. New York University,
      1963.

936   Lindberg, Arne O. Some recent changes in the vocabulary
      of the Swedish language. Ohio State University, 1952.

937   Lindemann, John W.R. Ge- as a preverb in late Old Eng-
       lish prose: Its meaning and function as suggested by a
       collation of West-Saxon, Mercian, and Northumbrian ver-
       sions of the Gospel according to Saint Matthew. Univer-
       sity of Wisconsin, 1957.

938   Lindsjo, Holger. A study of the Hebrew root שלב and
       its religious concepts. University of Chicago, 1940.

939   Lipton, Wallace S. The pronominal-intransitive alter-
       nation and its relationship to the transitive in Medieval
       French and Provencal. Yale University, 1957.

940   Lis, Anthony S. Attitudes and practices of executives
       and secretaries concerning disputable items of English
       usage in secretarial handbooks: A study made in the oil
       industry in Tulsa, Oklahoma. University of Minnesota,
       1961.

941   Lisker, Leigh. The [æ]-[ɛ] distinction: A problem in
       acoustic analysis. University of Pennsylvania, 1949.

942   Little, LeRoy. The syntax of vocalized pauses in spon-
       taneous cultivated speech. George Peabody College for
       Teachers, 1963.

943   Live, Anna H. Pre-history of Latin phonetic structure.
       University of Pennsylvania, 1959.

944   Llewellyn, Robert H. Adjective suffixes in Old Norse:
       A study in word-formation. Harvard University, 1946.

945   Lloyd, Paul M. A linguistic analysis of Old Spanish
       occupational terms. University of California at Berkeley,
       1960.

946   Locke, William N. The pronunciation of the French spoken
       at Brunswick, Maine. Harvard University, 1941.

947   Loewen, Jacob A. An introduction to Epera speech: Sambu
       dialect. University of Washington, 1958.

948   London, Gardiner H. Conjunctive adverbs in the prose
       texts of Alfonso X, The Learned. University of Wiscon-
       sin, 1951.

949   Long, Mary M. The English strong verb from Chaucer to
       Caxton. New York University, 1943.

950   Longacre, Robert E. Proto-Mixtecan. University of Penn-
       sylvania, 1955.

951   Longyear, Christopher R. Linguistically determined cate-
       gories of meaning: A comparative analysis of meaning in
       The Snows of Kilimanjaro in English and German. Univer-
       sity of Michigan, 1961.

952   Lopez-Morillas, Juan. El vocabulario y la dicción de
       Rubén Darío. University of Iowa, 1940.

953   Loth, Helen E. A study of the lexicography of the Casus
       Sancti Galli of Ekkehardus IV. University of Chicago,
       1937.

954   Loveless, Owen R. The Okinawan language: A synchronic
       description. University of Michigan, 1963.

955   Lowrey, Rosewell G. The English sentence in literature
       and in college freshman composition. George Peabody
       College for Teachers, 1927.

956   Lozano, Anthony G. A study of spoken styles in Colombian
       Spanish. University of Texas, 1964.

957   Lucke, Jessie R. A study of the Virginia dialect and its
       origin in England. University of Virginia, 1949.

958   Ludlum, Charles D., Jr. A critical commentary on the
       vocabulary of the Canterbury psalter. Stanford Univer-
       sity, 1954.

959   Luker, Benjamin F. The use of the infinitive instead of
       a finite verb in French. Columbia University, 1916.

960   Lukoff, Fred. A grammar of Korean. University of Penn-
       sylvania, 1954.

961   Lunceford, William M. The problem of the aorist parti-
       ciple in the New Testament. Southern Baptist Theological
       Seminary, 1952.

962   Lund, John J. The history of words pertaining to certain
       crafts in the principal Indo-European languages. Univer-
       sity of Chicago, 1932.

963   Lund, Wendell L. A study of the dialect of St. Editha
       and St. Etheldreda. Princeton University, 1933.

964   Lunt, Horace G., II.   The orthography of eleventh-century
      Russian manuscripts.   Columbia University, 1950.

965   Luper, John T., Jr.   Aorist tense in the writings of Luke.
      Southwestern Baptist Theological Seminary, 1934.

966   Lussky, George F.   Die mit dem Partizip des Präteritums
      umschriebenen Tempora im Altsächsischen.   University of
      Wisconsin, 1915.

967   Lyman, Rollo L.   English grammar in American schools be-
      fore 1850.   Columbia University, 1917.

968   Lynch, Charles A.   De verbis alienarum basium adiumento
      suppletis in lingua Graeca.   Harvard University, 1936.

969   Lynch, Irina B-M.   On Russian verbal voice: The -sja
      verbs.   Radcliffe College, 1955.

970   Lynn, Klonda.   A phonetic analysis of the English spoken
      by Mexican children in the elementary schools of Arizona.
      Louisiana State University, 1940.

971   Lyra, Franciszek.   English and Polish in contact.   Indi-
      ana University, 1962.

972   MacAdoo, Thomas O.   The modification of adjectives in
      Greek by means of prefixes.   University of Illinois, 1953.

973   MacCurdy, Raymond R., Jr.   The Spanish dialect in St.
      Bernard Parish, Louisiana.   University of North Carolina,
      1948.

974   Macdonald, Roderick R.   Russian prepositions.   Yale Uni-
      versity, 1955.

975   MacGran, Miles.   The prose vocabulary of Old French.   Uni-
      versity of Texas, 1959.

976   MacLeish, Andrew.   Patterns in the late East Midland sub-
      ject-verb cluster: A quantitative synchronic description.
      University of Wisconsin, 1961.

977   MacRae, Allan A.   Semitic proper names from Nuzi.   Univer-
      sity of Pennsylvania, 1936.

978   Macris, James.   An analysis of English loanwords in New
      York City Greek.   Columbia University, 1955.

979 Madden, John F. Studies in word-frequencies in Anglo-
     Saxon poetry. Harvard University, 1953.

980 Magers, Mildred K. The development of the grammatical
     use of word-order for relationships expressed by the
     accusative, with special reference to its development
     in subordinate clauses. University of Michigan, 1944.

981 Magner, Thomas F. Consonantal present stems in Slavic.
     Yale University, 1950.

982 Magnusson, Walter L. A genetic classification of the
     dialects of Ancient Greek. Columbia University, 1964.

983 Mahoney, Sister Catherine of Siena. Rare and late nouns,
     adjectives, and adverbs in St. Augustine's De civitate
     Dei: A morphological and semasiological study. Catholic
     University of America, 1935.

984 Malécot, André C. The influence of the consonantal en-
     vironment of the French mute -e upon its stability.
     University of Pennsylvania, 1952.

985 Malik, Joe, Jr. The origin of the Slavic week and the
     Slavic names for the days of the week. University of
     Pennsylvania, 1955.

986 Malone, Sister Helen D. An analysis and evaluation of
     phonemic differences in the speech of boys and girls
     at the kindergarten, first, second, and third grade
     levels. University of Michigan, 1954.

987 Malone, Kemp. Studies in English phonology. University
     of Chicago, 1919.

988 Mann, Sister M. Emmanuel. The clausulae of St. Hilary.
     Catholic University of America, 1936.

989 Manning, Clarence A. A study of archaism in Euripides.
     Columbia University, 1915.

990 Manning, Rev. Joseph M. The contribution of Dom Jean
     Mabillon, O.S.B., to the science of palaeography. Ford-
     ham University, 1950.

991 Mantinband, James H. An index of tense-stems and for-
     mants in cognate verbs of representative Indo-European
     languages. New York University, 1953.

992   Manzanares Cirre, Manuela. Los estudios arabes en España
      en el siglo XIX. University of Michigan, 1958.

993   Marchand, James W. The sounds and phonemes of Wulfila's
      Gothic. University of Michigan, 1955.

994   Marckwardt, Albert H. The origin and extension of the
      voiceless preterit and past participle inflections of the
      English irregular weak verb conjugation. University of
      Michigan, 1933.

995   Markley, James G. The verbal categories of substandard
      Spanish. University of Illinois, 1954.

996   Marten, Anita E. The morphophonemics of the Winnebago
      verbal. University of Wisconsin, 1964.

997   Martin, John W. Objective criteria of syntax and the
      determination of authorship in Spanish literature: A
      study of the method and its validity. University of
      Washington, 1956.

998   Martin, Raymond A. The syntax of the Greek of Jeremiah.
      Princeton Theological Seminary, 1957.

999   Martin, Samuel E. Morphophonemics of standard colloquial
      Japanese. Yale University, 1950.

1000 Mase, Sadi J. Aspects of Old Russian law and its termi-
      nology. Harvard University, 1952.

1001 Masters, Harry V. A study of spelling errors: A critical
      analysis of spelling errors occurring in words commonly
      used in writing. University of Iowa, 1927.

1002 Matejka, Ladislav. Reported speech in contemporary writ-
      ten standard Russian. Harvard University, 1961.

1003 Matson, Dan M. A grammatical sketch of Juang, a Munda
      language. University of Wisconsin, 1964.

1004 Matteson, Esther L. The Piro (Arawak) language. Univer-
      sity of California at Berkeley, 1963.

1005 Matthews, G. Hubert. Handbook of Siouan languages. Uni-
      versity of Pennsylvania, 1958.

1006 Mattingly, Michael G. A word index of Polydore Vergil's
      twenty-sixth book of the History of England, with brief
      syntactical studies. University of Ohio, 1934.

1007   Maxwell, Harry J. The syntactical and semantic usages
       of sollen in contemporary German. Stanford University,
       1964.

1008   Mayer, Edgar N. Processes of adoption of French loan-
       words into literary Russian in the latter eighteenth
       century: A study in bilingualism. Harvard University,
       1952.

1009   McCain, John W. Certain aspects of John Heywood's vo-
       cabulary in relation to his cultural interests. Univer-
       sity of North Carolina, 1938.

1010   McCartney, Eugene S. Figurative uses of animal names
       in Latin and their application to military devices: A
       study in semantics. University of Pennsylvania, 1911.

1011   McCarus, Ernest N. Descriptive analysis of the Kurdish
       of Sulaimaniya, Iraq. University of Michigan, 1956.

1012   McCobb, Arthur L. The double preterit forms gie-gienc,
       lie-liez, vie-vienc in Middle High German. Johns Hop-
       kins University, 1917.

1013   McCormick, Rev. John P. A study of the nominal syntax
       of indirect discourse in Hegesippus. Catholic Univer-
       sity of America, 1935.

1014   McCulloch, Donald F. A morphological study of the verb
       in Old French. New York University, 1959.

1015   McCulloch, James A. A lexicographical study of Apuleius'
       Cupid and Psyche. University of Pittsburgh, 1952.

1016   McCullough, Norman V. The morphology of John Bunyan,
       including observations of syntax, grammar and style with
       special reference to the King James Bible. Western Re-
       serve University, 1958.

1017   McDavid, Virginia G. Verb forms of the north central
       states and upper midwest. University of Minnesota, 1956.

1018   McDowell, David F. The nature of Old Spanish vocabulary
       as determined by an etymological and semantic analysis
       of the verbs in the prima parts of the General Estoria
       of Alfonso el Sabio. University of North Carolina, 1943.

1019   McElroy, Estelle L. Alexander Melville Bell--elocution-
       ist and phonetician. Columbia University, 1951.

1020 McGee, Alan V. The geographical distribution of Scandi-
      navian loan-words in Middle English. Yale University,
      1940.

1021 McGrady, Harold J., Jr. Verbal and nonverbal functions
      in school children with speech and language disorders.
      Northwestern University, 1964.

1022 McIntosh, Lois. A description and comparison of question
      signals in spoken English, Mandarin Chinese, French, and
      German for teachers of English as a second language. Uni-
      versity of Michigan, 1953.

1023 McJimsey, George D. Topographic terms in Virginia. Col-
      umbia University, 1939.

1024 McJimsey, Ruth B. Chaucer's irregular -e: A demonstra-
      tion among monosyllabic nouns of the exceptions to gram-
      matical and metrical harmony. Columbia University, 1942.

1025 McKaughan, Howard P. The inflection and syntax of Maranao
      verbs. Cornell University, 1957.

1026 McKibben, William T. Nonlocal uses of in with the accusa-
      tive in Apuleius. University of Chicago, 1942.

1027 McLaughlin, John C. A graphemic-phonemic study of a
      Middle English manuscript: MS Cotton Nero A.x. Indiana
      University, 1961.

1028 McLaurin, Eugene W. The influence of Hebrew and Classi-
      cal, Septuagint, and Hellenistic Greek elements in the
      redemptive terms of the Greek New Testament. University
      of Texas, 1952.

1029 McLemore, James S. The tradition of the Latin accent.
      University of Virginia, 1912.

1030 McMahon, L. Grammatical analysis as part of understand-
      ing a sentence. Harvard University, 1963.

1031 McMillan, James B. Phonology of the standard English of
      east central Alabama. University of Chicago, 1946.

1032 McMullen, Edwin W., Jr. English topographic terms in
      Florida, 1563-1874. Columbia University, 1950.

1033 McNamee, Rev. Maurice B. Francis Bacon's attitude toward
      grammar and rhetoric in the light of tradition. St. Louis
      University, 1945.

1034   McSweeney, Mariam J.   Word usage techniques in spelling.
       Boston University, 1959.

1035   McWilliams, Ralph D.   The adverb in colloquial Spanish.
       University of Illinois, 1952.

1036   Meadows, Gail K.   The development of Vulgar Latin hiatus
       groups in the Romance languages.   Harvard University,
       1944.

1037   Meadows, Leon R.   A study of the teaching of English
       composition in teachers' colleges in the United States,
       with a suggested course of procedure.   Columbia Univer-
       sity, 1928.

1038   Meikle, Herbert G.   A glossary of Colombian colloquial-
       isms (based on the speech of Colombian males).   Univer-
       sity of Michigan, 1961.

1039   Melamed, Judith T.   An experiment in sound discrimination
       in English and Thai.   Indiana University, 1962.

1040   Memming, Gerrit H.R.   Niederdeutsche 'Vörloopvertellsels',
       mit besonderer Rücksicht auf Ostfriesland.   University
       of Illinois, 1935.

1041   Mendeloff, Henry.   The evolution of the conditional sen-
       tence contrary to fact in Old Spanish.   Catholic Univer-
       sity of America, 1960.

1042   Mendenhall, George E.   The verb in early Northwest Semitic
       dialects.   Johns Hopkins University, 1947.

1043   Mendenhall, John C.   Aureate terms: A study of the liter-
       ary diction of the fifteenth century.   University of
       Pennsylvania, 1919.

1044   Menk, Edgar A.   The position of the possessive pronoun
       in Cicero's orations.   University of Iowa, 1925.

1045   Menyuk, Paula.   Syntactic structures in the language of
       children: Nursery school and first grade.   Boston Uni-
       versity, 1961.

1046   Meroney, Howard M.   Old English upp, uppe, uppan, and
       upon.   University of Chicago, 1943.

1047   Mersand, Joseph.   Scientific studies in Chaucer's Ro-
       mance vocabulary.   New York University, 1934.

1048   Merzbach, Herbert.   The phonological theory of the school
       of Prague: An exposition and revision.   University of
       Minnesota, 1953.

1049   Meskill, Robert H.   A transformational analysis of Turk-
       ish syntax.   University of Texas, 1964.

1050   Messing, Gordon M.   De consonantibus quae laryngophoni
       vocantur, praecipae quod ad linguam Graecam attinet.
       Harvard University, 1942.

1051   Metcalf, George J.   Forms of address in German (1500-
       1800).   Harvard University, 1935.

1052   Metlen, Michael.   Does the Gothic Bible represent idio-
       matic Gothic?   An investigation based primarily on the
       use of the present participle in the Gothic Bible.
       Northwestern University, 1932.

1053   Metzenthin, Esther M.   Die Länder- und Völkernamen im
       altislandischen Schrifttum.   Bryn Mawr College, 1935.

1054   Meyer, Christine L.   A semantic survey of certain verbs
       indicating departure and arrival in the Romance lan-
       guages.   University of Ohio, 1941.

1055   Meyer, George A.   The Latin suffix -aticus in Old French
       and in Spanish.   Yale University, 1934.

1056   Meyer, Herman C.   The authorship of the Old High German
       Tatian: Addition and non-addition of pronoun subjects.
       University of Chicago, 1937.

1057   Meyer, Robert T.   A chapter in English lexicography.
       University of Michigan, 1944.

1058   Meyers, Oliver T.   Phonology, morphology, and vocabulary
       in the language of Juan del Encina.   Columbia Univer-
       sity, 1961.

1059   Meyerstein, Goldie R.P.   Selected problems of bilingual-
       ism among immigrant Slovaks.   University of Michigan,
       1959.

1060   Meyerstein, Rud S.   A positional determination of seman-
       tic equivalences in French, English, and German.   Uni-
       versity of Michigan, 1955.

1061 Micklesen, Lew R. A morphological analysis of the modern
      Russian verb. Harvard University, 1951.

1062 Miele, Alfonse R. Armed forces language training in
      peacetime (since World War II). Columbia University,
      1958.

1063 Miller, Edward F. The influence of Gesenius on Hebrew
      lexicography. Columbia University, 1927.

1064 Miller, Raymond D. Secondary accent in modern English
      verse: Chaucer to Dryden. Johns Hopkins University,
      1904.

1065 Miller, Robert L. The linguistic relativity principle
      and Humboldtian ethno-linguistics: A history and ap-
      praisal. University of Michigan, 1963.

1066 Miller, Robert P. The particles in the dialogue of Yuan
      drama. Yale University, 1952.

1067 Miller, Roy A. Problems in the study of Shuo-wen Chieh-
      tzu. Columbia University, 1953.

1068 Miller, Wick R. The Acoma language. University of Cali-
      fornia at Berkeley, 1962.

1069 Miller, Wray. An analysis of the New Testament vocabu-
      lary. University of Pittsburgh, 1944.

1070 Miller, Wray. Diminutives in the New Testament. South-
      ern Baptist Theological Seminary, 1954.

1071 Milligan, Thomas R. The German verb-genitive locution
      from Old High German to the present: A study in struc-
      ture of content. New York University, 1960.

1072 Mills, Dorothy A. A descriptive analysis of the morphol-
      ogy of the diminutives ito, illo, ico, uelo, and of their
      increments (including feminine and plural forms) as used
      in Spanish America. University of Southern California,
      1955.

1073 Milnes, Humphrey N. Über die erotische Sprache in der
      mittelhochdeutschen höfischen Dichtung. University of
      Ohio, 1950.

1074   Mindel, Nissan. Sefer Liqqutei Amarim (Tanya), by Rabbi
        Schneur Zolman, translated, with an introduction and
        biography of the author. Columbia University, 1962.

1075   Minor, Charles B. An analytical study of grammatical
        uses and tendencies in some Restoration playwrights of
        comedies with comparison to present-day usages and
        tendencies. University of Denver, 1957.

1076   Minshall, Robert. The archaic characteristics of the
        West Germanic languages as opposed to the innovative
        tendencies of the North and East Germanic languages.
        Princeton University, 1952.

1077   Mockler, William E. The surnames of Trans-Allegheny,
        Virginia. Ohio State University, 1955.

1078   Mohr, Ernest. Analogy and its effect upon the evolution
        of the German strong verb. New York University, 1950.

1079   Mohr, Eugene V. Morphology and syntax of AB, a dialect
        of early Middle English. University of California at
        Berkeley, 1964.

1080   Monroe, James T. Main currents in Spanish Arabism (18th
        century to the present). Harvard University, 1964.

1081   Monson, Samuel C. Representative American phonetic
        alphabets. Columbia University, 1953.

1082   Montgomery, Thomas A. A linguistic study of the Book
        of Matthew in Manuscript I.I.6 of the Escorial Library.
        University of Wisconsin, 1955.

1083   Moon, Emma L. A metrical study of the three successive
        versions of Gervais de Basere's Lycoris, with special
        attention to the observance of the principles of Mal-
        herbe. University of Michigan, 1940.

1084   Moorefield, Allen S. The infinitive as accusative in
        modern Spanish. University of Southern California,
        1957.

1085   Moran, William L. A syntactical study of the dialect
        of Byblos as reflected in the Amarna tablets. Johns
        Hopkins University, 1950.

1086   Morgan, Raleigh, Jr. A lexical and semantic study of
        Old French jogleor and kindred terms. University of
        Michigan, 1952.

1087   Morine, Harold. A proposal for the teaching of linguis-
       tics in grades four, five, and six. Columbia University,
       1962.

1088   Morris, Walton. The syntax of the dative case in Aris-
       tophanes. Johns Hopkins University, 1960.

1089   Morton, Ermel J. A descriptive grammar of Tongan (Poly-
       nesian). Indiana University, 1962.

1090   Moseley, William W. An etymological vocabulary of the
       Spanish in the works of Gil Vicente. University of
       New Mexico, 1954.

1091   Moses, Elbert R., Jr. Palatography: A critical study
       and analysis of sound-image contacts. University of
       Michigan, 1936.

1092   Most, Rev. William G. The syntax of the Vitae sanctorum
       Hiberniae. Catholic University of America, 1946.

1093   Motherwell, George M. Old English morphemic structures:
       A grammatical restatement. Indiana University, 1959.

1094   Moutsos, Demetrius. A stratification of a segment of
       the modern Greek vocabulary. University of Chicago,
       1962.

1095   Mueller, Eugen H. Die Sprache Paul Flemings. Univer-
       sity of Minnesota, 1938.

1096   Mueller, Sister Mary M. The vocabulary of Pope St. Leo
       the Great. Catholic University of America, 1942.

1097   Muldowney, Sister Mary S. Word-order in the works of
       Saint Augustine. Catholic University of America, 1937.

1098   Muller, Daniel H. A study of the effects on pronunci-
       ation and intonation of accompanying audio-lingual drill
       with exposure to the written word. University of Cali-
       fornia at Berkeley, 1963.

1099   Muller, Henri F. Origine et histoire de la préposition
       à dans les locutions du type de faire quelque chose à
       quelqu'un. Columbia University, 1912.

1100   Munro, Edwin C. An etymological vocabulary of military
       terms in the works of Alfonso X. University of Wis-
       consin, 1950.

1101   Munzinger, Karl F. Studies in the psychology of lan-
       guage. University of Chicago, 1918.

1102   Murphy, Paul R. De lingua antiqua Illyrica. Harvard
       University, 1942.

1103   Murphy, Spencer L. A description of noun suffixes in
       colloquial Mexican Spanish. University of Illinois,
       1950.

1104   Murray, Rev. Joseph P. A selective English-Old French
       glossary as a basis for studies in Old French onoma-
       tology and synonymics. Catholic University of America,
       1951.

1105   Murray, Robert J. The use of conditional sentences in
       Saint John Chrysostom's homilies on the Gospel of Saint
       John. University of North Carolina, 1960.

1106   Myers, Abraham L. The use of the adjective as a sub-
       stantive in Horace. University of Pennsylvania, 1919.

1107   Myers, Jacob. The linguistic and literary form of the
       Book of Ruth. Johns Hopkins University, 1946.

1108   Myers, Melvin K. The verbal categories in colloquial
       literary French. University of Illinois, 1955.

1109   Myers, Oliver T. Phonology, morphology, and vocabulary
       in the language of Juan del Encina. Columbia Univer-
       sity, 1961.

1110   Naik, Manappa. Kannada, Literary and Colloquial: A
       study of two styles. Indiana University, 1964.

1111   Naoumides, Mark. Greek lexicography in the papyri.
       University of Illinois, 1961.

1112   Narváez, Richard A. A descriptive analysis of word for-
       mation in Old Spanish. University of Minnesota, 1959.

1113   Nasr, Raja T. The phonological problems involved in the
       teaching of American English to native speakers of Leba-
       nese Arabic. University of Michigan, 1955.

1114   Nathanson, Yale S. An analysis of sounds and frequency
       words basic to a new method of corrective speech. Uni-
       versity of Pennsylvania, 1930.

1115 Nelson, Agnes D. A study of the English speech of the
      Hungarians of Albany, Livingston Parish, Louisiana.
      Louisiana State University, 1957.

1116 Nemser, William J. The interpretation of English stops
      and interdental fricatives by native speakers of Hun-
      garian. Columbia University, 1961.

1117 Neuberg, Frank J. Ugaritic and the Book of Isaiah.
      Johns Hopkins University, 1950.

1118 Neumann, Joshua H. American pronunciation according to
      Noah Webster. Columbia University, 1924.

1119 Newcomb, William B. Some tempo manifestations of the
      terminals of English. University of Wisconsin, 1960.

1120 Newhard, Margaret E. Spanish orthography in the thir-
      teenth century. University of North Carolina, 1960.

1121 Newlin, Nicholas. The language of Synge's plays: The
      Irish element. University of Pennsylvania, 1950.

1122 Newmark, Leonard D. An outline of Albanian (Tosk)
      structure. Indiana University, 1955.

1123 Newnan, Eva M. The Latinity of the works of Hrotsvit
      of Gandersheim. University of Chicago, 1937.

1124 Ney, James W. A morphological and syntactic analysis
      of English compositions written by native speakers of
      Japanese. University of Michigan, 1963.

1125 Nichols, Ann E. A syntactical study of Aelfric's trans-
      lation of Genesis. University of Washington, 1964.

1126 Nichols, Edward J. An historical dictionary of baseball
      terminology. Pennsylvania State University, 1939.

1127 Nichols, Edward W. The semantic variability and seman-
      tic equivalents of -oso- and -lento-. Yale University,
      1913.

1128 Nicholson, George A. English words with native roots
      and with Greek, Latin or Romance suffixes. University
      of Chicago, 1914.

1129 Nida, Eugene A. A synopsis of English syntax. Univer-
      sity of Michigan, 1943.

1130 Nishiwaki, Augustine H.   The Dharma-Samgraha: A new edi-
      tion with linguistic commentary. Catholic University of
      America, 1962.

1131 Noble, Shlomo. The survival of Middle High German and
      Early New High German words in current Judeo-German
      translations of the Bible. University of Ohio, 1940.

1132 Noonan, John P. A study of the influence of descriptive
      grammar on high school texts used in the Kansas school
      system. University of Denver, 1955.

1133 Nordmeyer, George. Morphology of diphthongal light
      series in Germanic. Yale University, 1934.

1134 Norman, Arthur M. A Southeast Texas dialect study. Uni-
      versity of Texas, 1955.

1135 Norwood, Lotte. Êre and Scande: Eine Untersuchung der
      Wortbedeutung in vorhöfischer Zeit. University of Wis-
      consin, 1958.

1136 Noss, Richard B. An outline of Siamese grammar. Yale
      University, 1954.

1137 Nuner, Robert D. The verbal system of the Agallamh na
      Senórach. Harvard University, 1958.

1138 Nuñez, Benjamin. Términos topográficos en la Argentina
      colonial (1516-1810). Columbia University, 1957.

1139 Nye, Gertrude E. The phonemes and morphemes of Modern
      Persian: A descriptive study. University of Michigan,
      1955.

1140 Nye, Irene. Sentence connection, illustrated chiefly
      from Livy. Yale University, 1911.

1141 Nyerges, Anton H. Phonemics of Namdal Lapp. Indiana
      University, 1952.

1142 Obrecht, Dean H. Effects of the second formant in the
      perception of velarization in Lebanese Arabic. Univer-
      sity of Pennsylvania, 1961.

1143 O'Brien, Sister Mary B. Titles of address in Christian
      Latin epistolography to 543 A.D. Catholic University
      of America, 1930.

1144 Odenkircher, Carl J. The consonantism of the later
      Latin inscriptions: A contribution to the 'Vulgar Latin'
      question. University of North Carolina, 1952.

1145 O'Donnell, James F. The vocabulary of the letters of
      St. Gregory the Great: A study in late Latin lexico-
      graphy. Catholic University of America, 1934.

1146 O'Donnell, Roy C. The relationship between awareness
      of structural relationships in English and ability in
      reading comprehension. George Peabody College for
      Teachers, 1961.

1147 Oelschläger, Victor R.B. A preliminary Spanish word
      list of first appearances up to Berceo. University of
      Wisconsin, 1937.

1148 O'Grady, Geoffrey N. Nyaŋumaṭa grammar. Indiana Uni-
      versity, 1963.

1149 O'Hare, Thomas J. The linguistic geography of eastern
      Montana. University of Texas, 1964.

1150 Oinas, Felix J. The development of the postpositional
      cases in Balto-Finnic languages. Indiana University,
      1952.

1151 Oliphant, Robert T. The Latin-Old English glossary in
      the British Museum MS Harley 3376. Stanford University,
      1962.

1152 Olmstead, David L. The phonology of Polish. Cornell
      University, 1950.

1153 Olson, Paul R. Nominal suffixes in sixteenth-century
      Spanish. Harvard University, 1959.

1154 O'Mara, J. Francis. A comparison of the vocabulary of
      eight series of first grade readers. University of
      Connecticut, 1962.

1155 Ondis, Lewis A. Phonology of the Cilentan dialect, with
      a word index and dialect texts. Columbia University,
      1932.

1156 O'Neill, Agnes. The pre-Socratic use of ψυχή as a term
      for the principle of motion. Catholic University of
      America, 1915.

1157   Oney, Earnest R.   The Indo-European character of Hiero-
       glyphic Hittite: Phonology.   University of Chicago, 1951.

1158   Oppermann, Frederick W.   The Old Saxon vowel phonemes
       under medial and weak stress in the M manuscript of the
       Heliand.   University of Texas, 1959.

1159   Orbeck, Anders.   Early New England pronunciation as re-
       flected in some seventeenth-century town records of
       eastern Massachusetts.   Columbia University, 1927.

1160   Orne, Jerrold.   A Middle French vocabulary of building
       arts and trades.   University of Chicago, 1940.

1161   Orrick, Allan H.   A history of the generic names for the
       Germanic settlers in the British Isles.   Johns Hopkins
       University, 1956.

1162   Osborn, Henry A., Jr.   Warao phonology and morphology.
       Indiana University, 1962.

1163   Osinski, Sister M. Lucilla.   A study of structures of
       coordination in a representative sample of the Bio-
       graphia Literaria.   Catholic University of America,
       1963.

1164   Oswald, Victor A.   The phones of a Lehigh County dialect
       of Pennsylvania German.   Columbia University, 1949.

1165   Oswalt, Robert L.   A Kashaya grammar.   University of
       California at Berkeley, 1961.

1166   Ota, Akira.   Tense and aspect of present-day American
       English.   University of Michigan, 1962.

1167   Otten, Robert T.   Metron, mesos, and kairos: A semasio-
       logical study.   University of Michigan, 1957.

1168   Owen, George H.   An analysis of the phonemes of English
       speech, with instructional materials for teaching them
       to non-English speaking persons.   Wayne State University,
       1958.

1169   Oxtoby, Willard G.   Some inscriptions of the Safaitic
       Beduin.   Princeton University, 1962.

1170   Oyler, John E.   The compound noun in Harsdörffer's
       Frauenzimmer Gesprächspiele.   Northwestern University,
       1957.

1171   Pacaluyko, Ella. The verbal stem suffix -<u>nu</u>. Harvard
        University, 1963.

1172   Paff, William J. The geographical and ethnic names in
        the <u>Thithriks</u> saga: A study in the Old Germanic heroic
        legend. Harvard University, 1950.

1173   Palermo, Joseph A. The dialect of Villalba and its bear-
        ing on the problem of the Latinity of Sicily. Princeton
        University, 1950.

1174   Palmer, Rupert E., Jr. Thomas Whythorne's speech: A
        study of English pronunciation in the sixteenth century.
        Yale University, 1957.

1175   Paluszak, Rev. Anthony B. The subjunctive in the letters
        of St. Augustine. Catholic University of America, 1935.

1176   Panunzio, Wesley C. A study in Liégeois phonetics. Har-
        vard University, 1957.

1177   Panzer, Vern A. Trends in the articulation of English
        between American high schools and colleges, 1875-1958.
        University of Michigan, 1964.

1178   Pap, Leo. Portuguese-American speech: An outline of
        speech conditions among Portuguese immigrants in New
        England and elsewhere in the United States. Columbia
        University, 1949.

1179   Paper, Herbert H. The phonology and morphology of royal
        Achaemenid Elamite. University of Chicago, 1952.

1180   Pappageotes, George C. The phonomorphic element *-<u>wo</u>-
        in Indo-European. Columbia University, 1955.

1181   Paratore, Angela. Spanish verb phrase and clause struc-
        ture. Cornell University, 1950.

1182   Pardoe, T. Earl. A historical and phonetic study of
        Negro dialect. Louisiana State University, 1937.

1183   Parker, Gary J. Ayacucho Quechua grammar. Cornell Uni-
        versity, 1964.

1184   Parker, Kelvin M. A classified vocabulary of the <u>Cronica
        troyana</u>. University of Chicago, 1953.

1185 Parker, Mary-Braeme. A study of the speech of the Nan-
      ticoke Indians of Indian River Hundred, Sussex County,
      Delaware. Louisiana State University, 1954.

1186 Paryski, Marie. A study of Greek loan-words in the
      Sahidic and Bohairic dialects of the Coptic language.
      University of Michigan, 1941.

1187 Pascasio, Emy M. A descriptive-comparative study pre-
      dicting interference and facilitation for Tagalog speak-
      ers in learning English noun-head modification patterns.
      University of Michigan, 1960.

1188 Paternost, Joseph. The Slovenian verbal system: Morpho-
      phonemics and variations. Indiana University, 1963.

1189 Pattanayak, Debi P. A controlled historical reconstruc-
      tion of Oriya, Assamese, Bengali, and Hindi. Cornell
      University, 1961.

1190 Pazuniak, Natalia I. The vocative case in Ukrainian.
      University of Pennsylvania, 1956.

1191 Pearce, Ruth L. Month names in Lithuanian and Lettish.
      University of Pennsylvania, 1949.

1192 Pearson, Eleanor V. Loans in Old West Norse poetry.
      Yale University, 1952.

1193 Pederson, Lee A. The pronunciation of English in metro-
      politan Chicago: Vowels and consonants. University of
      Chicago, 1964.

1194 Pei, Mario A. The language of the eighth-century texts
      in northern France: A study of the original documents.
      Columbia University, 1932.

1195 Peng, Frederick C. A grammatical analysis of standard
      Chinese. State University of New York at Buffalo, 1964.

1196 Percival, Walter K. A grammar of Toba-Batak. Yale Uni-
      versity, 1964.

1197 Pérez, Raoul M. Vocabulario clasificado de Kalila et
      Digna. University of Chicago, 1942.

1198 Perry, Mary F. Linguistics as a basis for literary
      criticism. Indiana University, 1964.

1199 Peters, Robert A. A study of Old English words for
      'demon' and 'monster' and their relation to English
      place-names. University of Pennsylvania, 1961.

1200 Petersen, Phillip B. A linguistic study of the Old
      Leonese Fuero de Ledesma. University of California at
      Berkeley, 1956.

1201 Peterson, Gordon E. The significance of various por-
      tions of the wave length in the minimum duration neces-
      sary for the recognition of vowel sounds. Louisiana
      State University, 1939.

1202 Phillips, Rev. Leo T. The subordinate, temporal, causal,
      and adversative clauses in the works of St. Ambrose.
      Catholic University of America, 1937.

1203 Piccus, Jules. Expressions for color in Old Spanish
      poetry. Princeton University, 1951.

1204 Piche, Robert L., Sr. A study of certain syntactic
      elements in the Songs and Sonnets of John Donne. Cath-
      olic University of America, 1952.

1205 Pickett, Velma B. The grammatical hierarchy of Isthmus
      Zapotec. University of Michigan, 1959.

1206 Picon, Leon. A linguistic analysis of the Sinuhe Ro-
      mance. Dropsie College, 1952.

1207 Pierce, Adeline. Rhythm in literature parallels the
      scale of specificity in speech development. University
      of Michigan, 1940.

1208 Pierce, Joe E. A statistical study of consonants in
      New World languages. Indiana University, 1957.

1209 Piffard, Guérard. Philological considerations of La
      Chançun de Willame. Stanford University, 1957.

1210 Pike, Kenneth L. A reconstruction of phonetic theory.
      University of Michigan, 1942.

1211 Pillai, S. Agesthialangom. A generative grammar of
      Tamil. Indiana University, 1963.

1212 Pillsbury, Paul W. A demonstration of the applicability
      of descriptive linguistic techniques to discourse re-
      corded in literary contexts: Problems in the morphology
      and syntax of eleventh-century English nouns. University
      of Michigan, 1961.

1213   Pimsleur, Paul. French radio speech. Columbia University, 1956.

1214   Pincus, Michael S. An etymological lexicon of Ysopete Hystoriado. University of North Carolina, 1961.

1215   Pitkin, Harvey. Wintu grammar. University of California at Berkeley, 1963.

1216   Pittman, Richard S. A grammar of Telelcingo (Morelos) Nahuatl. University of Pennsylvania, 1953.

1217   Plant, Helmut R. Syntaktische Studien zu den Monseer Fragmenten; ein Beitrag zur inneren Form des Althochdeutschen. University of Cincinnati, 1964.

1218   Plassmann, Thomas B. The signification of $b^e r\bar{a}k\bar{a}$: A semasiological study of the Semitic stem b-r-k. Catholic University of America, 1910.

1219   Podgurski, Joseph C. The evolution of Latin finis in Old French. New York University, 1941.

1220   Poduska, Donald M. Synonymous verbs of motion in Plautus. Ohio State University, 1963.

1221   Politzer, Frieda N. A study of dialectalization in eighth-century Italian Vulgar Latin documents. Columbia University, 1954.

1222   Politzer, Robert L. A study of the language of eighth-century Lombardic documents. Columbia University, 1949.

1223   Pollock, Rafael A. Dialogue and transformation. Yale University, 1954.

1224   Pope, Marvin H. The Ugaritic particles w, p, and m, with excursus on b, l, and k. Yale University, 1949.

1225   Porter, Mary G. A dictionary of personal names in the Eddic poems (Elder Edda and Eddica Minora). University of North Carolina, 1960.

1226   Poss, Richard H. The articular and anarthrous constructions in the Epistle of James. Southwestern Baptist Theological Seminary, 1948.

1227   Postal, Paul. Some syntactic rules in Mohawk. Yale University, 1962.

1228   Poston, Lawrence S., Jr. An etymological vocabulary to
       The Celestina, A-E. University of Chicago, 1938.

1229   Potter, Edward E. The dialect study of Northwestern
       Ohio: A study of a transition area. University of
       Michigan, 1955.

1230   Poultney, James W. The syntax of the genitive case in
       Aristophanes. Johns Hopkins University, 1934.

1231   Pound, Glenn M. Phonological distortion in spoken secret
       languages: A consideration of its nature and use. Indi-
       ana University, 1964.

1232   Powell, James D. The personal pronoun in the Oxford MS
       of the Perlesvaus. University of Chicago, 1940.

1233   Powell, Richard M. Syncope and like phenomena in Ital-
       ian. Columbia University, 1954.

1234   Powers, Oscar S. Studies in the commercial vocabulary
       of early Latin. University of Chicago, 1941.

1235   Praninskas, Jean. The processes and patterns of trade
       name creation. University of Illinois, 1963.

1236   Pratola, Daniel J. Portuguese words of Italian origin.
       University of California at Berkeley, 1952.

1237   Premner, Ellen L. A glossary of sea terms in the Old
       Venetian portolani. University of Illinois, 1961.

1238   Prendergast, Sister M. Agnes C. The Latinity of the
       De vita contemplativa of Julianus Pomerius. Catholic
       University of America, 1938.

1239   Preuninger, Rosamunde M. The words for 'will, desire,
       seek, like, choose', and 'demand' in the Old German
       dialect. Brown University, 1941.

1240   Proulx, Pierre. Ugaritic verse structure and the poetic
       syntax of proverbs. Johns Hopkins University, 1956.

1241   Pugh, William L. The strong verb in Chaucer. Harvard
       University, 1911.

1242   Puhvel, Jaan. Laryngeals and the Indo-European verb.
       Harvard University, 1959.

1243 Pulgram, Ernst. The theory of proper names. Harvard University, 1946.

1244 Purczinsky, Julius O., Jr. A historical study of the Spanish segmental phoneme system. University of Texas, 1957.

1245 Purdy, Strother B. The language of Henry James. University of Wisconsin, 1960.

1246 Purves, Pierre M. Non-Semitic proper names from Nuzi. University of Pennsylvania, 1936.

1247 Pyles, Thomas. A history of the pronunciation of learned Latin loan-words and foreign words in English. Johns Hopkins University, 1938.

1248 Quinn, John J. The minor Latin-Old English glossaries in MS Cotton Cleopatra A III. Stanford University, 1956.

1249 Rabel, Lili E. Khasi, a language of Assam. University of California at Berkeley, 1958.

1250 Rael, Juan B. A study of the phonology and morphology of New Mexican Spanish based on a collection of 410 folk tales. Stanford University, 1937.

1251 Rainbow, Raymond, Jr. A linguistic study of Wynnere and Wastoure and Parlement of the Three Ages. University of Chicago, 1960.

1252 Raiter, Gladys W. Phonology and morphology of the Auchinleck Sir Tristram. Northwestern University, 1935.

1253 Ramacciotti, Sister M. Dominic. The syntax of Il fiore and of Dante's Inferno as evidence in the question of the authorship of Il fiore. Catholic University of America, 1936.

1254 Ramanujan, Attipat K. A generative grammar of Kannada. Indiana University, 1963.

1255 Ramirez, Manuel D. A study of the style and vocabulary of prose fiction of Valle-Inclán. University of North Carolina, 1959.

1256 Randolph, E.E. The -ing words in English, with special reference to the present participle. University of North Carolina, 1907.

1257   Rauch, Irmengard P.   The Old High German diphthongiza-
       tion: A description of a phonemic change. University
       of Michigan, 1963.

1258   Raven, Fritjof A.   The weak verb in Notker Labeo.
       George Washington University, 1944.

1259   Reaman, George E.   A method of teaching English to for-
       eigners. Cornell University, 1920.

1260   Rebsamer, Frederich R.   The position of the English ad-
       verb in relation to subject, verb, and object, 1400-
       1600. Columbia University, 1962.

1261   Reed, Carroll E.   The Pennsylvania German dialect spoken
       in the counties of Lehigh and Berks: Phonology and mor-
       phology. Brown University, 1941.

1262   Reed, David W.   The history of inflectional n in English
       verbs. University of Michigan, 1949.

1263   Regenos, Graydon W.   The Latinity of the Epistolae of
       Lupus of Ferrières. University of Chicago, 1937.

1264   Reibel, David A.   A grammatical index to the compound
       nouns of Old English verse (based on the entries in
       Grein-Köhler Sprachschatz d. a.-s. Dichter). Indiana
       University, 1963.

1265   Reichard, Gladys A.   Wiyot grammar and texts. Columbia
       University, 1926.

1266   Reid, James R.   The expression of future time from Indo-
       European to Romance. Harvard University, 1944.

1267   Reiff, Donald G.   A characterization-evaluation system
       for theories of Spanish verb morphology. University of
       Michigan, 1963.

1268   Reinmuth, Harry G.   Abstract terms in Notker's Boethius:
       A semantic and etymological study. Northwestern Univer-
       sity, 1938.

1269   Reining, Charles.   A study of verbs compounded with aus,
       ein, etc., as contrasted with those compounded with
       heraus, hinaus, herein, hinein, etc. Leland Stanford
       University, 1915.

1270   Renfroe, Walter J., Jr.   The relationship between the
       development of modern language teaching and textbooks
       in the United States in the twentieth century, with
       special reference to French.   Columbia University, 1963.

1271   Rettger, James F.   The development of the ablaut in the
       strong verbs of the East Midland dialects of Middle Eng-
       lish.   Yale University, 1932.

1272   Rettig, John W.   The Latinity of Martin of Braga.   Ohio
       State University, 1963.

1273   Rhyme, Orestes P.   A special class of mixed preterites
       in Middle High and Modern German.   Johns Hopkins Uni-
       versity, 1913.

1274   Rice, Allan L.   Gothic prepositional compounds in their
       relation to their Greek originals.   University of Penn-
       sylvania, 1932.

1275   Rich, Carroll Y.   An aural-oral experiment in freshman
       English.   Louisiana State University, 1962.

1276   Richards, John F.C.   De dialecto Milesia.   Harvard Uni-
       versity, 1934.

1277   Richards, Sumner E.   An experimental study of second-
       language comprehension.   Harvard University, 1956.

1278   Richmond, Winthrop E.   Place names in the English and
       Scottish popular ballads and their American variants.
       University of Ohio, 1947.

1279   Ricketson, Robert F.   Ablative after διά.   Southwestern
       Baptist Theological Seminary, 1944.

1280   Ringo, Elbert W.   The position of the noun modifier in
       colloquial Mexican Spanish.   University of Illinois,
       1951.

1281   Rivers, Gertrude B.   A study of the poetical vocabulary
       of Percy Bysshe Shelley.   Cornell University, 1939.

1282   Robe, Stanley L.   A dialect and folkloristic study of
       texts recorded in Los Altos of Jalisco, Mexico.   Univer-
       sity of North Carolina, 1950.

1283   Roberts, Aaron H.   Frequencies of occurrence of segmental
       phonemes in American English.   University of Wisconsin,
       1961.

1284   Roberts, Kimberley S. Orthography, phonology, and word-
       study of the Leal Conselheiro. University of Pennsyl-
       vania, 1940.

1285   Roberts, Paul M. The influence of Sir Walter Scott on
       the vocabulary of the modern English language. Univer-
       sity of California at Berkeley, 1948.

1286   Roberts, Ruth E. Welsh place-names in the earliest
       Arthurian texts. Columbia University, 1957.

1287   Robinson, David F. Uses of grammatical person in the
       novels of Andrej Belyj. University of Pennsylvania,
       1964.

1288   Robinson, Henry B. Syntax of the participle in the
       Apostolic Fathers in the edition of Gebhardt-Harnack-
       Zahn. University of Chicago, 1907.

1289   Rodeck, Herbert A.F. Das Adjektiv in den gesammelten
       Gedichten Gottfried Kellers. Johns Hopkins University,
       1941.

1290   Rodeffer, John D. The inflection of the English present
       plural indicative, with special reference to the Northern
       dialect. Johns Hopkins University, 1903.

1291   Rogers, Cleon L., Jr. A study of the Greek words for
       'righteousness'. Dallas Theological Seminary and Grad-
       uate School of Theology, 1962.

1292   Rogers, Francis M. The pronunciation of the Madeira and
       Azores dialects as compared with standard Portuguese.
       Harvard University, 1940.

1293   Romeo, Luigi. The economy of diphthongization in Early
       Romance. University of Washington, 1960.

1294   Rose, Harold D. A semantic analysis of time, with a
       semantic alphabet of the commonest English words. Indi-
       ana University, 1933.

1295   Rose, Jesse L. The durative and aoristic tenses in
       Thucydides. Duke University, 1938.

1296   Rose, Rial N. The semantic development of the Germanic
       verbs *geban, *saljan and *geldan. University of Vir-
       ginia, 1950.

1297   Rosen, Harold.   Old High German prepositional compounds
       in relation to their Latin originals.   University of
       Pennsylvania, 1933.

1298   Rosen, Karl M.D.   Greek loans in Latin through the period
       of the Republic.   Yale University, 1960.

1299   Rositzke, Harry A.   The speech of Kent before the Norman
       conquest.   Harvard University, 1935.

1300   Rossell, William H.   A grammar of the dialects of the
       Aramaic incantation texts.   Dropsie College, 1949.

1301   Rossi, Pietro C.   Derivatives of Latin fac in Italian,
       Spanish, and French: A study in semantics.   University
       of California, 1941.

1302   Roth, Hazel M.   Vowel tonality.   University of Iowa,
       1924.

1303   Rouillard, Zelda J.R.   An analysis of some patterns of
       comparison in the Matter of England romances.   Columbia
       University, 1960.

1304   Rowland, William T.   On the position in the clause of
       ne and ut in certain documents of colloquial Latin.
       Columbia University, 1918.

1305   Rozenberg, Martin S.   The stem s̆pt-: An investigation
       of biblical and extra-biblical sources.   University of
       Pennsylvania, 1963.

1306   Rubenstein, Herbert.   A comparative study of morpho-
       phonemic alternations in standard Serbo-Croatian, Czech
       and Russian.   Columbia University, 1950.

1307   Ruff, Edgar T.   The suffix -iste in French.   University
       of Texas, 1941.

1308   Ruíz, Macario B.   Weighting and sequencing English tense-
       aspect modifications for Hiligaynon speakers.   University
       of California at Los Angeles, 1963.

1309   Ruiz y Ruiz, Lina A.   A tentative Portuguese dictionary
       of dated first occurrences in certain documents between
       1351-1450.   University of Pennsylvania, 1964.

1310   Rushford, Rev. Martin S.   A phonological and semasio-
       logical comparison and commentary on a select religious

vocabulary in the Latin text and Old English version of Bede's Ecclesiastical History of the English Nation. St. John's University, 1942.

1311   Russell, Rev. Joseph W.   Scipio Maffei and Latin palaeography.   Fordham University, 1957.

1312   Russo, Harold J.   Morphology and syntax of the Leal Conselheiro.   University of Pennsylvania, 1939.

1313   Ruzic, Raiko H.   The verbal aspects in Serbo-Croatian. University of California, 1938.

1314   Ryberg, Josef E.   Separable prefixes in Cruciger's adaptations of Luther's sermons.   University of Illinois, 1956.

1315   Ryder, Frank G.   Verb-adverb compounds in Gothic and Old High German.   University of Michigan, 1950.

1316   Sachs, Abraham J.   Prolegomena to a grammar of Middle Assyrian.   Johns Hopkins University, 1939.

1317   Sackrin, Gene M.   An analysis of Modern French vocalic patterns, 1884-1953: A functional-structural survey. Columbia University, 1955.

1318   Sacks, Norman P.   The Latinity of the dated documents in the Portuguese territory.   University of Pennsylvania, 1940.

1319   Sadler, J.D.   A linguistic study of Excidium Troiae. University of Texas, 1951.

1320   Sáez, Mercedes.   Puerto Rican-English phonotactics. University of Texas, 1962.

1321   Sa'id, Majed F.   Lexical innovation through borrowing in Modern Standard Arabic.   Princeton University, 1964.

1322   Saitz, Robert L.   Functional word order in Old English subject and object patterns.   University of Wisconsin, 1955.

1323   Salom, Alwyn P.   Some problems of syntax in New Testament Greek.   University of Chicago, 1957.

1324   Salus, Peter H.   The compound noun in Indo-European: A survey.   New York University, 1963.

1325   Salzmann, Zdenek. A sketch of Arapaho grammar. Indiana
       University, 1963.

1326   Samarin, William J. The Gbeya language. University of
       California at Berkeley, 1962.

1327   Samilov, Michael. The phoneme <u>jat'</u> in Slavic. Columbia
       University, 1960.

1328   Sanford, Carlisle. The addresses of Hebrews. Dallas
       Theological Seminary and Graduate School of Theology,
       1962.

1329   Sapir, Edward. The Takelma language of southwestern
       Oregon. Columbia University, 1909.

1330   Sapon, Stanley M. A study of the development of the
       interrogative in Spanish from the twelfth through the
       fifteenth centuries. Columbia University, 1951.

1331   Saporta, Sol. Morpheme alternates in Spanish. Univer-
       sity of Illinois, 1955.

1332   Sarot, Eden E. Folklore of the dragonfly: A linguistic
       approach. Princeton University, 1949.

1333   Sas, Louis F. The noun declension system in Merovingian
       Latin. Columbia University, 1937.

1334   Sastri, Madugula I. Kernel sentence types in Wulfstan's
       homilies. Western Reserve University, 1962.

1335   Satterthwait, Arnold C. Parallel sentence-construction
       grammars of Arabic and English. Harvard University,
       1962.

1336   Savage, David J. Old English scholarship in England,
       1800-1840. Johns Hopkins University, 1935.

1337   Sawyer, Janet B.M. A dialect study of San Antonio,
       Texas: A bilingual community. University of Texas, 1957.

1338   Sawyer, Jesse O., Jr. Achinese historical phonology.
       University of California at Berkeley, 1959.

1339   Schabacker, John M. A study of the position of the verb
       in the German subordinate clause. New York University,
       1952.

1340   Schachter, Paul M.   A contrastive analysis of English
       and Pangasinan.   University of California at Los Ange-
       les, 1960.

1341   Schaeffer, Rudolf F.   An English-Latin-Greek derivative
       lexicon.   Columbia University, 1951.

1342   Schappelle, Benjamin F.   The German dialect in Brazil:
       Colonies and dialect.   University of Pennsylvania, 1917.

1343   Schenker, Alexander.   Polish nominal inflection.   Yale
       University, 1953.

1344   Scherer, Philip.   Germanisch-baltoslavische Wortglei-
       chungen.   Yale University, 1935.

1345   Schick, George V.   The stems dûm and damám in Hebrew.
       Johns Hopkins University, 1912.

1346   Schieman, Sister M. Bernard.   The rare and late verbs
       in St. Augustine's De civitate Dei: A morphological and
       semasiological study.   Catholic University of America,
       1938.

1347   Schlatter, Edward B.   The development of the vowel of
       the unaccented initial syllable in Italian.   University
       of Wisconsin, 1909.

1348   Schlueter, Rudolph J.   Das Fremdwort bei Grimmelshausen.
       University of Wisconsin, 1934.

1349   Schmalstieg, William R.   Criteria for the determination
       of Slavic borrowings in Lithuanian.   University of Penn-
       sylvania, 1956.

1350   Schmalz, Guenter G.   Zur Geschichte des Wortes 'Verein'.
       Ohio State University, 1952.

1351   Schnerr, Walter J.   Modern Portuguese uses of ser and
       estar.   University of Pennsylvania, 1947.

1352   Schnieders, Marie H.   Die einheimischen nicht kompo-
       nierten schwachen Verben der jan- und on- Klasse im
       Altnordischen.   Bryn Mawr College, 1935.

1353   Scholes, Robert J.   Grammaticality of phonemic strings,
       with reference to prevocalic consonant clusters in
       American English.   Indiana University, 1964.

1354   Schrader, Helen W.   A linguistic approach to the study
       of rhetorical style. Northwestern University, 1949.

1355   Schramm, Gene M.   Judeo-Baghdadi: A descriptive analysis
       of the Colloquial Arabic of the Jews of Baghdad. Dropsie
       College, 1956.

1356   Schultz, Martin C.   A preliminary investigation of the
       acoustical characteristics of inter-phonemic transitions.
       University of Iowa, 1955.

1357   Schulz-Behrend, George. Das Fremdwort in der Verssprache
       Arno Holz. University of Iowa, 1945.

1358   Schütz, Albert J.   A dialect survey of Viti Levu. Cor-
       nell University, 1962.

1359   Schwabe, Henry O.   The semantic development of words for
       'eating' and 'drinking' in the Germanic dialects. Uni-
       versity of Chicago, 1913.

1360   Schwartz, Stephen P.   The pre-Latin dialect of Aquitania
       between the Pyrenees and the Garonne (except Bordeaux).
       Harvard University, 1962.

1361   Schwesinger, Gladys C.   The social-ethical significance
       of vocabulary. Columbia University, 1926.

1362   Scott, Charles T.   A linguistic study of Persian and
       Arabic riddles: A language-centered approach to genre
       definition. University of Texas, 1963.

1363   Scott, Ralph W.   A study of the uses of the prepositions
       ab, apud, and cum in the Formulae Marculfi, the Formulae
       andecavenses, the Cartae senonicae and the Lex salica.
       Columbia University, 1938.

1364   Scott-Thomas, Lois M.   The vocabulary of Benjamin Frank-
       lin. University of Chicago, 1927.

1365   Scottron, Edith M.   The development of the Latin passive
       verb in the Romance languages. Columbia University,
       1949.

1366   Scribner, Rev. Simon.   Figures of word-repetition in the
       first book of Sir Philip Sidney's Arcadia. Catholic
       University of America, 1948.

1367   Seago, Dorothy W. An analysis of language factors in intelligence tests. Johns Hopkins University, 1924.

1368   Seale, Lea L. Indian place-names in Mississippi. Louisiana State University, 1939.

1369   Sears, Robert S. Syntactical studies in Heinrich Mann. University of Illinois, 1954.

1370   Sears, Vaudrey W. The use of the future tense in the New Testament. Southern Baptist Theological Seminary, 1950.

1371   Sebeok, Thomas A. Finnish and Hungarian case systems: Their form and function. Princeton University, 1945.

1372   Sebuktekin, Hikmet I. Turkish-English contrastive analysis: Turkish morphology and corresponding English structures. University of California at Berkeley, 1964.

1373   Sechrist, Frank K. The psychology of unconventional language. Clark University, 1913.

1374   Sehrt, Edward H. Die Formen der Konjunktion und im Westgermanischen. Johns Hopkins University, 1915.

1375   Seiden, William. Havasupai phonology and morphology. Indiana University, 1963.

1376   Seifert, Lester W.J. The Pennsylvania German dialect spoken in the counties Lehigh and Berks: Vocabulary. Brown University, 1941.

1377   Selcke, Benno H. A comparative study of the syntax of the infinitive in the Old Germanic languages. Northwestern University, 1940.

1378   Seltzer, Harriett A. The development of the function word system from Vulgar Latin to modern Spanish. University of Illinois, 1950.

1379   Semaan, Khalil I. Phonetics in early Islam: The speech sounds. Columbia University, 1959.

1380   Senior, Judith. The concepts of parts of speech in the early grammars of the Spanish language. Radcliffe College, 1956.

1381 Seright, Orin D. Syntactic structures in Keats' poetry.
      Indiana University, 1964.

1382 Serruys, Paul L-M. Prolegomena to the study of the
      Chinese dialects of Han time according to Fang yen.
      University of California at Berkeley, 1956.

1383 Seymour, Richard K. Nominal word formation by suffixes
      in the Swabian dialect. University of Pennsylvania,
      1956.

1384 Shah, Iris S. An investigation of linguistic decision
      points and encoding segments in spoken English. Cor-
      nell University, 1960.

1385 Shannon, Alice A. A descriptive syntax of the Parker
      manuscript of the Anglo-Saxon Chronicle from 734 to
      891. University of Michigan, 1962.

1386 Shawcross, John T. Milton's spelling, its biographical
      and critical implications. New York University, 1958.

1387 Shawkat, Mahmoud H. A descriptive grammar of educated
      Damascene Arabic. Cornell University, 1962.

1388 Sheets, Louis A. Wulfstan's prose: A reconsideration.
      Ohio State University, 1964.

1389 Shefts, Betty J. Pānini 3.1.68-85: A study in the pro-
      cedure of the Indian grammarians. Yale University, 1955.

1390 Sheldon, Esther K. Standards of pronunciation according
      to the grammarians and orthoepists of the sixteenth,
      seventeenth, and eighteenth centuries. University of
      Wisconsin, 1938.

1391 Shelley, Percy V. English and French in England, 1066-
      1100. Pennsylvania State University, 1914.

1392 Shepston, Howard F. A vocabulary of the Livre rouge d'eu.
      Harvard University, 1940.

1393 Sherlock, Richard B. The syntax of the nominal forms of
      the verb, exclusive of the participle, in St. Hilary.
      Catholic University of America, 1948.

1394 Sherman, Dorothy H. A study of the influence of vowels
      on recognition of adjacent consonants. University of
      Iowa, 1952.

1395   Shetter, William Z., Jr.   Umlaut in medieval Dutch non-
       literary texts.   University of California at Berkeley,
       1955.

1396   Shewmake, Edwin F.   English pronunciation in Virginia.
       University of Virginia, 1920.

1397   Shipley, William F.   Maidu grammar.   University of Cali-
       fornia at Berkeley, 1959.

1398   Shoemaker, Alfred L.   Studies on the Pennsylvania Ger-
       man dialect of the Amish community in Arthur, Illinois.
       University of Illinois, 1940.

1399   Sholes, George N.   Transformations in French grammar.
       University of Indiana, 1958.

1400   Shook, Lawrence K.   Aelfric's Latin Grammar: A study in
       Old English grammatical terminology.   Harvard University,
       1940.

1401   Shott, Hugh I., II.   An analysis of uninflected connec-
       tives and its use as a teaching device.   University of
       Denver, 1957.

1402   Shoup, June E.   The phonemic interpretation of acoustic-
       phonetic data.   University of Michigan, 1964.

1403   Shupe, Eldon E., Jr.   An evaluation of remedial English
       at Flint Junior College, 1957-58.   University of Mich-
       igan, 1959.

1404   Shuy, Roger W.   The boundary between the Northern and
       Midland dialects in Illinois.   Western Reserve Univer-
       sity, 1962.

1405   Sibayan, Bonifacio P.   English and Iloko segmental pho-
       nemes.   University of Michigan, 1961.

1406   Siefert, George J., Jr.   Meter and case in the Latin
       elegiac pentameter.   University of Pennsylvania, 1948.

1407   Silva-Fuenzalida, Ismael.   Papiamentu morphology.   North-
       western University, 1952.

1408   Simon, Evelyn H.   The language of Richard Wagner's li-
       brettos, with special reference to Middle High German
       and other archaic elements.   New York University, 1952.

1409   Simpson, Claude M., Jr.   The English speech of early
       Rhode Island, 1636-1700.   Harvard University, 1936.

1410   Singh, Jag D.   Grammatical structure of Bangru.   Uni-
       versity of Pennsylvania, 1959.

1411   Siracusa, Joseph.   A comparative study of syntactic
       redundancy in Italian and Spanish.   University of Illi-
       nois, 1962.

1412   Sirich, Edward J.   A study in the syntax of Alexandre
       Hardy.   Johns Hopkins University, 1914.

1413   Sitachitta, Kanda.   English aural and oral tests for
       Thai students at the high school level.   Georgetown
       University, 1964.

1414   Sjoberg, Andrée F.C.   The phonology of a Telugu dialect.
       University of Texas, 1957.

1415   Skahill, Rev. Bernard H.   The syntax of the _variae_ of
       Cassiodorus.   Catholic University of America, 1935.

1416   Skelton, Robert B.   A spectrographic analysis of Spanish
       vowel sounds.   University of Michigan, 1950.

1417   Skiles, J.W.D.   The Latinity of Arbeo's _Vita Sancti
       Corbiniani_ and of the revised _Vita et actus Beati
       Corbiniani espiscopi Frigisingensis aecclesiae_.   Uni-
       versity of Chicago, 1939.

1418   Skillman, Billy G.   Phonological and lexical features of
       the speech of first generation native-born inhabitants
       of Cleburne County, Arkansas.   University of Denver,
       1953.

1419   Skilton, John.   The translation of the New Testament
       into English, 1881-1900: Studies in language and style.
       University of Pennsylvania, 1961.

1420   Sladen, Charles F.   The approach of academic to spoken
       style in German.   University of Pennsylvania, 1917.

1421   Slaten, Arthur W.   Quantitative nouns in the Pauline
       Epistles and their translation in the revised version.
       University of Chicago, 1916.

1422   Sleator, Mary D.   Phonology and morphology of an American
       English dialect.   Indiana University, 1957.

1423   Sleeth, Charles R.   The sentence accent of the verb in
        the Indo-European.   Princeton University, 1941.

1424   Slobin, Dan I.   Grammatical transformations in childhood
        and adulthood.   Harvard University, 1963.

1425   Small, George W.   The comparison of inequality: The
        semantics and syntax of the comparative particle in
        English.   Johns Hopkins University, 1923.

1426   Smalley, William A.   Outline of Khmu structure.   Colum-
        bia University, 1956.

1427   Smeaton, Barnston H.   Lexical expansion due to technical
        change as illustrated by the Arabic of Al Hasa, Saudi
        Arabia, during the decade 1938-48.   Columbia University,
        1959.

1428   Smith, Alfred W.   Semantic shift of Teutonic noun cog-
        nates in English and German.   George Peabody College
        for Teachers, 1954.

1429   Smith, Charles L.   A Greek-Aramaic glossary of the vocab-
        ulary of Jesus in the Gospel of Mark.   Yale University,
        1947.

1430   Smith, Harley.   A recording of English sounds at three
        age levels in Ville Platte, Louisiana.   Louisiana State
        University, 1936.

1431   Smith, Harlie L., Jr.   The phonology of Arabic loanwords
        in Old Spanish.   University of Minnesota, 1953.

1432   Smith, Henry Lee, Jr.   The laryngeals and Germanic weak-
        grade vocalism.   Princeton University, 1938.

1433   Smith, Madorah E.   An investigation of the development
        of the sentence and the extent of vocabulary in young
        children.   University of Iowa, 1925.

1434   Smith, Maria W.   Studies in the syntax of the Gathas of
        Zarathushtra, together with text, translation, and notes.
        University of Pennsylvania, 1929.

1435   Smith, Nellie A.   The Latin element in Shakespeare and
        the Bible.   George Peabody College for Teachers, 1924.

1436   Smith, Philip H., Jr.   The syntactic uses of Indo-
        European verb reflexes in four daughter languages.
        University of Pennsylvania, 1960.

1437 Snortum, Niel K. Apo koinou and allied constructions
      in Middle English. Stanford University, 1956.

1438 Snyder, Warren A. A phonemic and morphemic analysis of
      Southern Puget Sound Salish. University of Washington,
      1957.

1439 Sobelman, Harvey. Structural analysis at the syntactic
      level. Harvard University, 1960.

1440 Soffietti, James P. Phonemic analysis of the word in
      Turinese, a Gallo-Italic dialect, by the acoustic
      approach, based on Jaberg and Jud's Linguistic Atlas
      of Italy and Southern Switzerland. Columbia University,
      1949.

1441 Solá, Donald F. Huánuco Kechua: The grammar of words
      and phrases. Cornell University, 1958.

1442 Soles, Myrtle. Studies in colloquial language in the
      poems of Catullus. University of Michigan, 1954.

1443 Sorvig, Ralph W. Topical analysis of Spanish loan-words
      in written American English of the American Southwest.
      University of Denver, 1952.

1444 Sotiropoulous, Demetrius. Noun morphology of modern
      Demotic Greek: A descriptive analysis. University of
      Michigan, 1963.

1445 Sousa, Thomas F. A linguistic analysis of a portion of
      the Galician translation of the General Estoria by
      Alfonso X, El Sabio. University of Wisconsin, 1964.

1446 Southern, Paul. The New Testament use of the preposition
      κατά, with special reference to its distributive as-
      pects. Southern Baptist Theological Seminary, 1949.

1447 Southworth, Franklin C., III. A test of the comparative
      method. Yale University, 1958.

1448 Spaulding, Robert K. History and syntax of the progres-
      sive constructions in Spanish. University of California,
      1925.

1449 Spiegel, Irving. Old Judaeo-Spanish evidence of Old
      Spanish pronunciation. University of Minnesota, 1952.

1450   Springer, George P. Soviet linguistic theory. Harvard
       University, 1954.

1451   Stabler, Lewis B. Initiatory study of Middle French
       syntax, with checklist. University of North Carolina,
       1935.

1452   Stanbury, Walter A. The language of Francis Quarles.
       Duke University, 1938.

1453   Standerwick, Henry F. Etymological studies in the Greek
       dialect inscriptions. Columbia University, 1932.

1454   Stankiewicz, Edward. The declension and gradation of
       substantives in contemporary standard Russian. Harvard
       University, 1954.

1455   Stanley, Oma. The speech of east Texas. Columbia Uni-
       versity, 1936.

1456   Staples, Charles L. Professional Latin in modern Eng-
       lish: A study on educational readjustment. Pennsylvania
       State University, 1912.

1457   Starr, Wendell R. Structural dislocation in the conver-
       sation of high school students. University of Minnesota,
       1958.

1458   Steadman, John M. The origin of the historical present
       in English. University of Chicago, 1916.

1459   Steger, Stewart A. American dictionaries. University
       of Virginia, 1913.

1460   Stehle, Dorothy. Sibilants and emphatics in South Ara-
       bic. University of Pennsylvania, 1940.

1461   Steiner, Mary F. An etymological study of Old Spanish
       personal names. Northwestern University, 1953.

1462   Steiner, Roger J. Two centuries of Spanish and English
       bilingual lexicography (1590-1798). University of
       Pennsylvania, 1963.

1463   Stenberg, Theodore T. The relation between the sentence
       and the paragraph. Cornell University, 1926.

1464   Stephens, James M., Jr. A structural analysis of Rho-
       danian speech. Yale University, 1954.

1465 Stephenson, Edward A. Early North Carolina pronunci-
      ation. University of North Carolina, 1958.

1466 Stern, Charlotte D. Studies on the Sayagués in the
      early Spanish drama. University of Pennsylvania, 1960.

1467 Stetkewycz, Jaroslav. Modern Arabic poetic and prose
      language. Harvard University, 1962.

1468 Stevens, Alan M. Madurese phonology and morphology.
      Yale University, 1964.

1469 Stevens, Linton C. La langue de Brantôme. University
      of Minnesota, 1936.

1470 Stevens, Martin. The language of the Towneley plays:
      A comparative analysis of the identical York and
      Towneley plays, the Caesar Augustus, the Talents and
      the Stanzas of the Wakefield Master. Michigan State
      University, 1956.

1471 Stevens, William John. Grammatical gender in MS Corpus
      Christi College Cambridge 402 and MS Bodley 34. Western
      Reserve University, 1959.

1472 Stevick, Earl W. Syntax of colloquial East Armenian.
      Cornell University, 1955.

1473 Stidson, Russell O. The use of ye in the function of
      thou in Middle English literature from MS Auchinleck to
      MS Vernon: A study of grammar and social intercourse in
      fourteenth-century England. Leland Stanford Junior Uni-
      versity, 1914.

1474 Stilwell, Robert S. A glossary for the Vercelli Prose
      Homilies. University of Texas, 1947.

1475 Stimson, Hugh M. The Chung-yüan yin yün: A study in an
      early Mandarin phonological system. Yale University,
      1959.

1476 Stockwell, Robert P. Chaucerian graphemics and phone-
      mics: A study in historical methodology. University of
      Virginia, 1952.

1477 Stoesser, Rose A. 'Le court d'amours' of Mahiu le
      Poriier: A fourteenth-century allegorical poem, edited
      with linguistic, historical, and literary introduction.
      University of California at Berkeley, 1959.

1478   Stone, Robert C. The language of Codex Bezae D. University of Illinois, 1936.

1479   St. Onge, Keith R. A quantitative method in the study of phonetic assimilation. University of Wisconsin, 1953.

1480   Stout, W.W. The progress of linguistic science before 1700. University of North Carolina, 1926.

1481   Stowe, Ancel R. English grammar schools in the reign of Elizabeth. Columbia University, 1909.

1482   Stowe, Arthur N. The syllable in linguistics and automatic speech recognition. Harvard University, 1958.

1483   Straubinger, O. Paul. Given names in German proverbs. University of California at Los Angeles, 1946.

1484   Strausbaugh, John A. The use of _auer a_ and _auer de_ as auxiliary verbs in Old Spanish from the earliest texts to the end of the thirteenth century. University of Chicago, 1934.

1485   Street, John C. The language of the Secret History of the Mongols. Yale University, 1955.

1486   Strickland, William E. The speech of the Aubigney-sur-Nére (Cher) region. University of North Carolina, 1950.

1487   Strong, Mabel E. A lexical study of Guy of Warwick. Cornell University, 1934.

1488   Strout, Clevy L. A linguistic study of the journals of the Coronado expedition. University of Colorado, 1958.

1489   Sturgis, James W. The second person singular of the Latin future indicative as an imperative. University of Oklahoma, 1910.

1490   Sturcken, Henry T., Jr. Studies in thirteenth-century Spanish syntax. University of North Carolina, 1953.

1491   Suárez, Emma G., and Suárez, Jorge A. A description of colloquial Guarani. Cornell University, 1961.

1492   Sublette, Edith B. The locative functions of _ser_ and _estar_ and some auxiliary functions of _ser_ and _haber_. University of Iowa, 1938.

1493   Subramoniam, Vadasery I. A descriptive analysis of a
        dialect of Tamil. Indiana University, 1958.

1494   Suelzer, Sister Mary J. The clausulae in Cassiodorus.
        Catholic University of America, 1944.

1495   Sugden, Herbert W. The grammar of Spenser's Faerie
        Queen. Duke University, 1933.

1496   Summey, George. Modern punctuation, its utility and
        conventions. Columbia University, 1919.

1497   Susskind, Norman. A history of French relative pronoun
        constructions. Yale University, 1957.

1498   Sutherland, Robert D. Language and Lewis Carroll. Uni-
        versity of Southern California, 1964.

1499   Swadesh, Mary H. A grammar of the Tunica language.
        Yale University, 1935.

1500   Swaim, Gerald G. A grammar of the Akkadian tablets
        found at Ugarit. Brandeis University, 1962.

1501   Swann, Harvey J. French terminologies in the making:
        Studies in conscious contributions to the vocabulary.
        Columbia University, 1918.

1502   Swanson, Donald C.E. The Greek and Sanskrit written
        accent. Princeton University, 1941.

1503   Swieczkowski, Walerian. Word order patterning in Middle
        English: A quantitative study based on Piers Plowman
        and Middle English sermons. Harvard University, 1958.

1504   Szamek, Pierre E. The eastern American dialect of
        Hungarian. Princeton University, 1947.

1505   Szklarczyk, Lillian G. Essai sur la structure phono-
        logique du français. University of Pennsylvania, 1961.

1506   Taha, Abdul K. The structure of two-word verbs in Eng-
        lish. University of Texas, 1958.

1507   Tallent, John B. An experimental evaluation of the
        teaching of English grammar by traditional and struc-
        tural methods. University of Tennessee, 1961.

1508   Tan, Jan C. English language teacher training in Indo-
        nesia. University of Michigan, 1962.

1509   Tappan, Robert L. Estudio lexicográfico del Poema de
       Fernán González con un índice completo de las frecuen-
       cias de los vocablos. Tulane University, 1954.

1510   Tarpley, Fred A. A word atlas of Northeast Texas.
       Louisiana State University, 1960.

1511   Taylor, George B. Verbal aspect in early Romance.
       Stanford University, 1952.

1512   Teeter, Karl V. The Wiyot language. University of
       California at Berkeley, 1962.

1513   Thomas, Dominic R. Oral language sentence structure
       and vocabulary of kindergarten children living in low
       socio-economic urban areas. Wayne State University,
       1962.

1514   Thomas, Earl W. The pronunciation of the Portuguese of
       central Minas Gerais. University of Michigan, 1947.

1515   Thomas, Lawrence L. The linguistic theories of N.J.
       Marr. University of California at Berkeley, 1954.

1516   Thomas, Russell. Syntactical processes involved in the
       development of the adnominal periphrastic genitive in
       the English language. University of Michigan, 1932.

1517   Thompson, Laurence C., Jr. A grammar of spoken South
       Vietnamese. Yale University, 1954.

1518   Tidwell, James N. The literary representation of the
       phonology of the Southern dialect. University of Ohio,
       1948.

1519   Tihany, Leslie C. The avowing of King Arthur: A morpho-
       logical and phonological study of the works in rime and
       of certain nonriming works. Northwestern University,
       1936.

1520   Tiller, Fritz. Structural problems of the first Ger-
       manic ablaut series. Yale University, 1940.

1521   Tinkler, John D. A critical commentary on the vocabu-
       lary and syntax of the Old English version in the Paris
       Psalter. Stanford University, 1964.

1522   Tjossem, Herbert K. New England pronunciation before
       1700. Yale University, 1956.

1523   Toconita, Michael J.   Three problems in contemporary
       French monolingual lexicography.   University of Pennsyl-
       vania, 1964.

1524   Toland, John M.   De vocalium mutatione illa apud Graecos
       antiquos quae hodie _sandhi_ dicitur.   Harvard University,
       1935.

1525   Topping, Donald M.   Chamorro structure and the teaching
       of English.   Michigan State University, 1963.

1526   Tosh, Leo W.   A linguistic interpretation of a model for
       the machine translation of German into English.   Univer-
       sity of Texas, 1962.

1527   Townsend, Charles E.   The language of the memoirs of
       Princess Natal'ja Borisovna Dolgorukaja.   Harvard Uni-
       versity, 1962.

1528   Trager, Edith C.   The Kiowa language: A grammatical
       study.   University of Pennsylvania, 1960.

1529   Trager, George L.   The use of the Latin demonstratives
       (especially _ille_ and _ipse_) up to 600 A.D., as the source
       of the Roman article.   Columbia University, 1932.

1530   Traver, Alice A.   The modificational patterns of the
       substantive head construction in present-day American
       English.   University of Michigan, 1945.

1531   Trittschuh, Travis E.   The semantics of political car-
       toon and slogan in America, 1876-1884.   Ohio State Uni-
       versity, 1952.

1532   Troike, Rudolph C.   A descriptive phonology and morphol-
       ogy of Coahuilteco.   University of Texas, 1959.

1533   Trotter, Julius C., Jr.   The use of the perfect tenses
       in the Pauline Epistles.   Southern Baptist Theological
       Seminary, 1951.

1534   Trusler, Margaret.   A study of the language of the
       Wakefield group in Towneley on the basis of significant
       rime-words, with comparison of forms within the line in
       both the Towneley and York plays.   University of Chicago,
       1933.

1535   Tschirwa, Bayara A.   Linguistic and stylistic problems
       of word order in modern Russian: The types of combination

of subject and verbal predicate. Radcliffe College, 1958.

1536 Tsevat, Matitiahu. A study of the language of the Biblical Psalms. Hebrew Union College, 1953.

1537 Tsiapera, Maria. A descriptive analysis of Cypriot Maronite Arabic. University of Texas, 1963.

1538 Tsuzaki, Stanley M. English influences in the phonology and morphology of the Spanish spoken in the Mexican colony in Detroit, Michigan. University of Michigan, 1963.

1539 Tuckerman, Charles S. Prolegomena to a diachronic study of subjunctive usage in Netherlandish. Harvard University, 1958.

1540 Tukey, Ann. Kinship terminology in the Romance languages. University of Michigan, 1962.

1541 Turner, Elbert D., Jr. The vocabulary of Bernal Díaz del Castillo's Historia verdadera de la Nueva España. University of North Carolina, 1950.

1542 Turner, Glen D. Jivaro phonology and morphology. Indiana University, 1958.

1543 Turville, Dorothy. French feminine singular nouns derived from Latin neuter plurals. Columbia University, 1925.

1544 Tweddell, Colin E. The Iraya (Mangyan) language of Mindoro, Philippines: Phonology and morphology. University of Washington, 1958.

1545 Tyler, Priscilla. Grammars of the English language to 1850, with special emphasis on school grammars used in America. Western Reserve University, 1954.

1546 Uhlfelder, Myra L. De proprietate sermonum vel rerum: A study and critical edition of an early medieval set of verbal distinctions. Bryn Mawr College, 1952.

1547 Uhrhan, Evelyn E. Linguistic analysis of Góngora's baroque style. University of Illinois, 1951.

1548 Underhill, Robert. Turkish verbal constructions. Harvard University, 1964.

1549   Ulvestad, Bjarne E.   Indirect discourse in Modern Ger-
       man: A structural analysis.   University of Wisconsin,
       1954.

1550   Uyechi, Roy Y.   A study of Ugaritic alphabetic personal
       names.   Brandeis University, 1961.

1551   Valdman, Albert.   A descriptive phonology of Standard
       French.   Cornell University, 1960.

1552   Valk, Melvin E.   Die Bedeutung des Verbalpräfixes ge-
       in Gottfried von Strassburg's Tristan.   University of
       Wisconsin, 1937.

1553   Van Campen, Joseph A.   Bulgarian conjugation.   Harvard
       University, 1961.

1554   Van der Velde, Sjoerd.   Loss of inflection in the Dutch
       language.   State University of Iowa, 1962.

1555   Van Nooten, Barend A.   Mahābhārata text analysis with
       the aid of the digital computer.   University of Cali-
       fornia at Berkeley, 1964.

1556   Van Riper, William R.   The loss of post-vocalic r in
       the eastern United States.   University of Michigan, 1958.

1557   Van Schoonveld, Cornelis.   Semantic analysis of the past
       predicates in Old Russian.   Columbia University, 1953.

1558   Van Syoc, Wayland B.   The phonology and morphology of
       the Sundanese language.   University of Michigan, 1959.

1559   Van Wagoner, Merrill Y.   A grammar of Iraqi Arabic.
       Yale University, 1945.

1560   Van Zandt-McCleary, J. Marie.   The Medulla Grammatice
       Latin-English dictionary: A diplomatic transcription.
       University of Chicago, 1959.

1561   Vaughan, Alden G.   Latin adjectives with partitive mean-
       ing in Republican literature.   University of Pennsylvania,
       1942.

1562   Veerhusen, Elsbeth.   Das Adjektiv in der Syntax Notkers.
       University of Wisconsin, 1903.

1563   Villegas, Francisco.   Glosario del argot costarricense.
       University of Michigan, 1953.

1564   Vilnay, Zev. Transformation of place-names in Palestine.
       Dropsie College, 1938.

1565   Voge, Noel A. Significant aspects of the morphology of
       the language of the archpriest Avvakum. University of
       California at Berkeley, 1953.

1566   von Raffler, Walburga. Studies in Italian-English bi-
       lingualism. Indiana University, 1953.

1567   von Schmertzing, Wolfgang P. Die deutsche Jägersprache
       bis zum Anfang des 16. Jahrhunderts. Harvard University,
       1938.

1568   Voogd, Henry. A critical and comparative study of the
       Old Latin of the First Book of Samuel. Princeton Theo-
       logical Seminary, 1947.

1569   Wahlgren, John H. A descriptive grammar of Russian
       chemical nomenclature. University of California at
       Berkeley, 1964.

1570   Waldorf, Norman O. The hapax legomena in the Old Eng-
       lish vocabulary: A study based upon the Bosworth-Toller
       dictionary. Stanford University, 1953.

1571   Walker, Francis C. Syntax of the infinitive in Shake-
       speare. Harvard University, 1911.

1572   Walker, James A. Adjective suffixes in Old English.
       Harvard University, 1948.

1573   Walker, Louisa V. Latin in current periodicals and
       newspapers. University of Wisconsin, 1923.

1574   Walker, Saunders E. A dictionary of the folk speech of
       the East Alabama Negro. Western Reserve University,
       1956.

1575   Walker, Willard B. Reference, taxonomy, and inflection
       in Zuni. Cornell University, 1964.

1576   Wallace, Betty J. A quantitative analysis of consonant
       clusters in present-day English. University of Michigan,
       1951.

1577   Walsh, Chad. The preposition at the end of a clause in
       early Middle English. University of Michigan, 1943.

1578   Walsh, James L.   Some aspects of medieval Spanish sibi-
       lants, as reflected in MS S of the Libro de buen amor.
       University of Illinois, 1963.

1579   Walsh, John V.   Prolegomena to the Hellenizing of the
       Phoenician alphabet.   Johns Hopkins University, 1948.

1580   Wang, William S-Y.   Phonemic theory A (with application
       to Midwestern English).   University of Michigan, 1960.

1581   Ward, Ralph L.   The relative chronology of the phonetic
       changes in primitive Greek.   Yale University, 1935.

1582   Ware, Elmer W.   A study in the tense of the Book of
       Revelation.   Southern Baptist Theological Seminary,
       1954.

1583   Warotamasikkhadit, Udom.   Thai syntax: An outline.
       University of Texas, 1963.

1584   Waterhouse, Viola G.   The grammatical structure of
       Oaxaca Chontal.   University of Michigan, 1958.

1585   Waterman, John T.   The phonology and morphology of the
       Low German passages in Gabriel Rollenhagen's Amantes
       amentes.   University of California at Los Angeles,
       1949.

1586   Waterman, Margaret B.   Surnames of the original settlers
       in Watertown, Massachusetts.   University of Wisconsin,
       1942.

1587   Watkins, Arthur R.   The function of the verbal prefix ge-
       in late Middle High German as exemplified in Die Erlösung.
       Stanford University, 1949.

1588   Watkins, Calvert W.   Studies in the Indo-European origins
       of the Celtic verb: I: The sigmatic aorist.   Harvard Uni-
       versity, 1959.

1589   Watson, John W., Jr.   A phonemic study of the Northum-
       brian dialect of Old English.   University of Virginia,
       1941.

1590   Way, Sister Agnes C.   The language and style of the
       letters of St. Basil.   Catholic University of America,
       1927.

1591 Weaver, Bill R. The forms and usage of the personal
      pronouns in Castigos e Documentos Para Bien Vivir
      Ordenados por el Rey Don Sancho IV. University of Wis-
      consin, 1964.

1592 Weaver, Ella H. An approach to language behavior from
      the point of view of general semantics. Northwestern
      University, 1950.

1593 Weber, Robert H. A comparative study of regional terms
      common to the Twin Cities and the Eastern United States.
      University of Minnesota, 1964.

1594 Wechter, Pinchos. Ibn Barun's book of comparison between
      the Hebrew and the Arabic languages. Dropsie College,
      1940.

1595 Weese, Walter E. Word-order as a factor of style in
      Chaucer's poetry. Yale University, 1951.

1596 Weidman, Robert H. A study of nominal compounds in Mid-
      dle High German, based on the Manesse manuscript. Uni-
      versity of Wisconsin, 1938.

1597 Weiman, Ralph W. Native and foreign elements in a lan-
      guage: A study of general linguistics applied to modern
      Hebrew. Columbia University, 1950.

1598 Weinberg, Harry L. A general semantics analysis of the
      Lysenko controversy and its ideological foundations.
      Northwestern University, 1953.

1599 Weinberger, Marvin E. The linguistic implications in
      the theory and poetry of Stéphane Mallarmé. Cornell
      University, 1956.

1600 Weinig, Mother Mary A. Syntax and rhetoric in T.S.
      Eliot's Four Quartets. Fordham University, 1957.

1601 Weinreich, Uriel. Research problems in bilingualism,
      with special reference to Switzerland. Columbia Uni-
      versity, 1951.

1602 Weinstein, David. A comparative study of the adequacy
      of selected vocabulary lists for simplifying Hebrew
      literature. Harvard University, 1956.

1603 Welch, John J. Latin initial syllables: An historical
      phonological study. University of Pennsylvania, 1962.

1604 Wells, Frederic L. Linguistic lapses, with especial reference to the perception of linguistic sounds. Columbia University, 1906.

1605 Wells, John C. The suffix -heit in Old High German and Old Low German: Its origin and its history to 1100 A.D. Harvard University, 1952.

1606 Welmers, William E. A descriptive grammar of Fanti, with vocabulary. University of Pennsylvania, 1943.

1607 Wente, Edward F. The syntax of verbs of motion in Egyptian. University of Chicago, 1959.

1608 Wentworth, Harold. Blendwords in English glossaries illustrative of linguistic growth. Cornell University, 1934.

1609 Werbow, Stanley N. Konjunktionale Adverbialsätze in oberdeutscher Unterhaltungsprosa des 15.-16. Jahrhunderts: Ein Beitrag zur stilistischen Syntax. Johns Hopkins University, 1953.

1610 Wescott, Roger W. A comparative grammar of the Albanian language: I. Phonology. Princeton University, 1948.

1611 Wesenberg, Thor G. A study of the conditional and the subjunctive in Provençal narrative poetry. Harvard University, 1925.

1612 Wetmore, Thomas H., Jr. The low-central and low-back vowels of the Eastern United States. University of Michigan, 1957.

1613 Whichard, Rogers D. The Norman dialect. University of North Carolina, 1946.

1614 White, Mother Elizabeth. A study of symmetrical and asymmetrical tendencies in the sentence structure of Sir Thomas Browne's Urne Buriall. Catholic University of America, 1962.

1615 White, Elliot A. The function of intonation in determining the expression values of the nasal interjections. University of Michigan, 1920.

1616 Whitesell, James E. Accented vowels in the Northumbrian dialect of Old English. Harvard University, 1935.

1617   Whitfield, Francis J.   The inflection of modern literary
       Russian.   Harvard University, 1944.

1618   Whitman, Robert H.   The morphology of the Svjatoslav
       Izbornik of 1073.   Harvard University, 1964.

1619   Whitted, Joseph W.   An etymological lexicon of the His-
       toria Troyana.   University of North Carolina at Chapel
       Hill, 1963.

1620   Whittemore, John H.   The syntax of Saint-Simon.   Yale
       University, 1956.

1621   Wiersmaz, Stanley M.   A linguistic analysis of words
       referring to monsters in Beowulf.   University of Wis-
       consin, 1961.

1622   Wilbur, Terence H.   A study of the magical vocabulary
       of common Germanic.   University of California at Berke-
       ley, 1954.

1623   Wilhelms, John W.   The language of Cicero's De legibus.
       University of Minnesota, 1942.

1624   Wilkins, George W., Jr.   Verbal categories of the Poema
       del Cid.   Tulane University, 1961.

1625   Wilkins, Mother Myrtle.   Word-order in selected sermons
       of the fifth and sixth centuries.   Catholic University
       of America, 1940.

1626   Willbern, Glenn D.   Vocabulary elements in thirteenth-
       century Castilian.   University of Chicago, 1941.

1627   Williams, Edna R.   The conflict of homonyms in English.
       Yale University, 1936.

1628   Williams, Hazel B.   A semantic study of some current,
       pejoratively regarded language symbols involving Negroes
       in the United States.   New York University, 1953.

1629   Williams, Mary A.   The intellectual vocabulary of German
       as a loan field.   Stanford University, 1949.

1630   Williams, Ronald J.   The morphology and syntax of Papyrus
       Insinger.   University of Chicago, 1948.

1631   Williamson, Juanita V.   A phonological and morphological
       study of the speech of the Negro of Memphis, Tennessee.
       University of Michigan, 1961.

1632   Williamson, Kay R.M.   A grammar of the Kolokuma dialect of Ijo.   Yale University, 1964.

1633   Willis, William H.   Compound words in Aeschylus.   Yale University, 1940.

1634   Wilson, Baxter D.   A comparative study of the initial consonant clusters of Old English and certain cognate languages.   University of Virginia, 1952.

1635   Wilson, Harry R.   The dialect of Lunenburg County, Nova Scotia: A study of the English of the county, with reference to its sources, preservation of relics, and vestiges of bilingualism.   University of Michigan, 1959.

1636   Wilson, Joseph B.   The passive voice in Old Icelandic. Stanford University, 1960.

1637   Wilson, L.R.   Chaucer's relative constructions.   University of North Carolina, 1905.

1638   Wilson, Marie A.S.   The language of Joseph of Arimathie. University of Chicago, 1951.

1639   Wilson, Marvin R.   Syntactical studies of future tenses in Sahidic.   Brandeis University, 1963.

1640   Wilt, Henry T.   Religio: A semantic study of pre-Christian use of the terms religio and religiosus.   Columbia University, 1954.

1641   Winburne, John N.   Word and phrasal patterns in current English.   Michigan State University, 1951.

1642   Winget, Lynn W.   Auxiliary verbs in the prose works of Alfonso X.   University of Wisconsin, 1960.

1643   Wingo, Elvis O.   Latin pronunciation in the Classical Age.   University of Illinois, 1963.

1644   Winter, Ralph D.   English function words and content words: A quantitative investigation.   Cornell University, 1953.

1645   Wintermute, Orval S.   Semitic loanwords appearing in Egyptian texts from the New Kingdom.   Johns Hopkins University, 1959.

1646   Wise, Alfred S., Jr.   Russian noun suffixation.   Yale University, 1953.

1647   Wolf, Carl U.   Toward an understanding of the vocaliza-
       tion of the pre-Massoretic Hebrew.   University of Hart-
       ford, 1942.

1648   Wolfe, Frank A.   An experimental study of a system in
       English grammar.   Temple University, 1964.

1649   Wolff, Gladys G.   French r: A study in historical pho-
       netics and phonemics.   Columbia University, 1958.

1650   Womack, William T.   A study of teachers' attitudes to-
       ward debatable items of English usage.   Columbia Univer-
       sity, 1957.

1651   Wood, Cecil.   A contribution to a system of skaldic
       word order.   Yale University, 1953.

1652   Wood, Frederic T.   The accentuation of nominal compounds
       in Lithuanian.   Princeton University, 1928.

1653   Woodard, Clement M.   Derivatives of caballus and equus
       in French and Provençal territory.   University of North
       Carolina, 1938.

1654   Woodbridge, Hensley C.   Spanish nautical terms of the
       Age of Discovery.   University of Illinois, 1951.

1655   Woodring, Maxie N.   A study of the quality of English
       in Latin translations.   Columbia University, 1925.

1656   Woods, Frank L.   Vocabulary studies of the Old High Ger-
       man Benedictine rule.   Yale University, 1952.

1657   Woolf, Henry B.   The Old Germanic principles of name-
       giving.   Johns Hopkins University, 1936.

1658   Worth, Dean S.   A contribution to the study of the syn-
       tactic binary combination in contemporary standard
       Russian.   Harvard University, 1956.

1659   Worthington, Martha G.   Proper names in the Guillaume
       d'Orange cycle: A supplement to the Table of Langlois.
       Tulane University, 1954.

1660   Wright, James E.   A Reuter phonology: Mecklenburg and
       Hochsprache vowel correspondence tables.   Brown Uni-
       versity, 1959.

1661   Yamagiwa, Joseph K.   The older inflected forms surviving
       in the modern Japanese written language.   University of
       Michigan, 1943.

1662 Yarmohammadi, Lotfollah. A contrastive study of modern
      English and modern Persian. Indiana University, 1964.

1663 Yarrow, Andrew H. Aberrant forms in the Mahābhārata.
      Yale University, 1950.

1664 Yates, Warren G. A descriptive study of the structural
      features indicating 'plurality' in the German noun as
      exemplified in Thomas Mann's novel Der Zauberberg.
      University of Michigan, 1956.

1665 Yedlicka, Brother Leo C. Expressions of the linguistic
      area of repentance and remorse in Old French. Catholic
      University of America, 1944.

1666 Yen, Isabella Y. A grammatical analysis of Syau Jīng.
      Cornell University, 1956.

1667 Yiu, Tung. The T'ai-shan dialect. Princeton University,
      1946.

1668 Yoder, Edward. The position of possessive and demon-
      strative adjectives in the Noctes atticae of Aulus
      Gellius. University of Pennsylvania, 1928.

1669 Yoder, J. Otis. New Testament synonyms in the Septuagint.
      Northern Baptist Theological Seminary, 1954.

1670 Yokoyama, Masako. The inflections of eighth-century
      Japanese. Yale University, 1949.

1671 Yorkey, Richard C. A study of the practical application
      of structural linguistics to the teaching of English in
      Lebanese elementary schools. University of Michigan,
      1960.

1672 Yotsukura, Sayo. A structural analysis of the usage of
      the articles in English. University of Michigan, 1963.

1673 Young, George A. Sentence patterns in Alfred's Orosius
      and the Latin original: A comparative study. Texas
      Technological College, 1964.

1674 Young, Norma D. Index verborum Silianus. University of
      Iowa, 1939.

1675 Zahn, Louis J. An etymological lexicon of El libro de
      los exemplos por A.B.C. University of North Carolina,
      1957.

1676   Zardoya, Maria C. España en la poesia americana. University of Illinois, 1952.

1677   Zebian, George J. The use of the ablative of quality and the ablative of respect in Latin literature. Johns Hopkins University, 1959.

1678   Zeitlin, Jacob. Accusative with infinitive and some kindred constructions. Columbia University, 1908.

1679   Zenn, Elizabeth G. The neuter plural in Latin lyric verse. University of Pennsylvania, 1947.

1680   Zeps, Valdis J. Latvian and Finnic linguistic convergences. Indiana University, 1961.

1681   Zide, Norman H. Korku phonology and morphology. University of Pennsylvania, 1960.

1682   Zidonis, Frank J. The role of linguistics in the high school English program. Ohio State University, 1961.

1683   Ziegler, Julian. Personal pronouns in the fifteenth century. New York University, 1953.

1684   Zimmer, Karl E. Degrees of productivity: Affixal negation in English and other languages. Columbia University, 1963.

1685   Zimmerman, Jane D. Radio pronunciations: A study of two hundred educated non-professional radio speakers. Columbia University, 1943.

1686   Zimmerman, Rev. Odo J. The Late Latin vocabulary of the Variae of Cassiodorus. Catholic University of America, 1943.

1687   Zipper, Eva M. An etymological glossary to the Old High German Tatian. New York University, 1960.

1688   Zrimc, Rudolf. Slovene conjugation as represented in the dialect of Ljubljana. Harvard University, 1961.

1689   Zucker, George K. Linguistic theory of the Siglo de Oro: An evaluation. State University of Iowa, 1964.

1690   Zúñiga-Tristán, Virginia. El anglicismo en la habla costarricense. Tulane University, 1958.

ADDENDA

1691   Andersen, Francis I.   Studies in Hebrew syntax.   Johns
       Hopkins University, 1960.

1692   Barrett, Madie W.   A phonology of Alabama speech.
       University of North Carolina, 1948.

1693   Berlin, Overton B.   The descriptive semantics of Tzeltal
       numeral classifiers.   Stanford University, 1964.

1694   Ching, Eugene.   A handbook for Chinese teachers of the
       English language.   Columbia University, 1959.

1695   Crabb, David W.   Nasal and nasalized roots in Proto-
       Southwest Bantu.   Columbia University, 1962.

1696   Durbin, Marshall E.   A componential analysis of Western
       Apache.   State University of New York at Buffalo, 1964.

1697   Glicksberg, Daniel.   Memory span in English as a foreign
       language.   University of Michigan, 1963.

1698   Griffin, David A.   Elementos mozárabes en el 'Vocabu-
       lista' atribuído a Ramón Martí.   University of Chicago,
       1956.

1699   Guanco, Nelia Rivera.   A descriptive-contrastive analysis
       of English and Tagalog verbs.   University of Michigan,
       1963.

1700   Haugen, Einar.   The early history of the New Norse move-
       ment in Norway.   University of Illinois, 1931.

1701   Hendon, Rufus S.   Phonology and morphology of Ulu Muar
       Malay.   Yale University, 1959.

1702   Hill, Archibald A.   Elizabethan translations from
       Spanish.   Yale University, 1927.

1703   Hollander, Lee M.   Prefixal s in Germanic.   Johns Hopkins
       University, 1905.

1704   Hollien, Harry F.   Some laryngeal correlates of vocal
       pitch.   University of Iowa, 1955.

1705 Holmes, Urban T. Unemphatic object pronouns in Old
      French. Harvard University, 1923.

1706 House, Arthur. Influence of consonantal environment
      upon the duration, frequency and intensity of vowels.
      University of Illinois, 1951.

1707 Kučera, Henry. Language policy in the Soviet Union.
      Harvard University, 1952.

1708 Kunst, Arthur E. Twenty-four versions of <u>Huckleberry
      Finn</u>: Studies in translation. Indiana University, 1961.

1709 Levine, Lewis. Speech variation and social structure
      in four North Indian villages. Columbia University,
      1959.

1710 Li, Fang Kuei. Mattole, an Athabaskan language. Uni-
      versity of Chicago, 1928.

1711 Maclay, Howard S. Language and non-linguistic behavior:
      An experimental investigation. University of New
      Mexico, 1956.

1712 Malmstrom, Jean. A study of the validity of textbook
      statements about certain controversial grammatical
      items in the light of evidence from the Linguistic
      Atlas. University of Minnesota, 1958.

1713 McCullough, Joe T. The Spanish of the Oriente Antio-
      queno (Colombia). University of California at Berkeley,
      1954.

1714 Newman, Stanley S. The Yokuts language of California.
      Yale University, 1932.

1715 Noll, J. Douglas. Perceptual significance of acoustic
      correlates of consonant voicing contrasts. University
      of Iowa, 1960.

1716 Parish, Charles. Twentieth-century criticism of form
      in <u>Tristram Shandy</u>. University of New Mexico, 1959.

1717 Peterson, Paul W. Dialect of Vercelli Book (Old Eng-
      lish). Columbia University, 1951.

1718 Plath, Warren J. Multiple-path syntactic analysis of
      Russian. Harvard University, 1964.

1719   Pooley, Robert C. Language and grammar in textbooks
       on English. University of Wisconsin, 1932.

1720   Puglisi, Elizabeth A. The bio-psychological deter-
       mination of the adequacy of informants in American
       English and Brazilian Portuguese. University of
       Michigan, 1954.

1721   Robinson, Fred C. Variations: A study in the diction
       of Beowulf. University of North Carolina at Chapel
       Hill, 1961.

1722   Roblin, Gloria L. A comparative analysis of trans-
       lation equivalence of connotative meaning for Tagalog
       and English speaking subjects. State University of
       New York at Buffalo, 1963.

1723   Running, Leona R. An investigation of the Syriac ver-
       sion of Isaiah. Johns Hopkins University, 1964.

1724   Rus, Louis C. Grammatical ambiguity in E.E. Cummings.
       University of Michigan, 1955.

1725   Schwartz, Benjamin. The root and its modification in
       Primitive Indo-European. Columbia University, 1945.

1726   Skendi, Stavro. Albanian and South Slavic oral poetry.
       Columbia University, 1951.

1727   Stevens, Cj. Early American phonology. Louisiana
       State University, 1954.

1728   Tucker, Robert W. Quantity and quality of vowels in
       Latin. Cornell University, 1929.

1729   Twaddell, W. Freeman. The periphrastic passive in
       Notker's German. Harvard University, 1930.

1730   Walker, Elna Laverne. Teaching English as a second
       language to Spanish-speaking adults. University of
       Texas, 1963.

1731   Wolff, Hans. Comparative phonology of the Siouan
       languages. Indiana University, 1949.

1732   Yegerlehner, John F. Phonology and morphology of
       Hopi-Tewa. Indiana University, 1957.

1733   Youngblood, Joseph E. Music and language: Some re-
       lated analytical techniques. Indiana University, 1960.

INDEX

INDEX